When Business is Sweet

Management Experiences and Guidelines

When Business is Sweet

Management Experiences and Guidelines

Colin Lyle

Memory Lane

First published in Great Britain by Memory Lane

ISBN 978-0-9563076-8-2

Typeset by TW Typesetting, Plymouth, Devon

Printed and bound in Great Britain by

CPI Antony Rowe, Chippenham and Eastbourne

For my family

Contents

Preface   xi

Introduction: the Family Business background   xiii

I   A Family Business Management   1

    1. The Lyle Family Sugar Business   1

    2. A Little Background: Sugar Refining   3

    3. Managing Cane Cultivation   5

    4. Is Your Product Unhealthy?   6

    5. Lyle's Golden Syrup: Quality Control   9

    6. Family Management   12

    7. Family Recruitment   16

    8. Family Promotion   17

II Technologies to Improve a Business   21

    9. Packeting Productivity in Town and Country   21

    10. Production Scheduling   24

    11. How to Halve Fuel Consumption   25

    12. Computer Hazards   27

    13. Operations Research: A Tale of the Unexpected   30

    14. Necessary Nitpickers   31

    15. Ideas for Management Organising   34

    16. Very Practical Statistical Techniques   36

    17. Management Consultants: Importing a Bomb Factory   38

    18. The Case for Consultants   39

    19. Training as an Investment   41

    20. Managerial Fashions   43

III Directing a Family (or Other) Business   45

    21. Family Directors Only?   45

    22. One Boss or Two?   46

    23. Changing Chairmen   49

    24. Non-Executive Directors: For and Against   50

    25. A Really Useful Director   53

    26. 'Acquired' Directors   54

    27. The Usefulness of Subsidiary Boards   56

    28. T & L's Board: Growth or Control?   57

    29. Seniors' Workload Problem   60

    30. 'Mission Impossible?'   62

    31. A Solution: the Chief of Staff System   63

    32. Practical Delegation: 'Divisional Directors'   65

IV **Home Grown Economics** 68

33. Arguments for Private Enterprise 68

34. Private Wealth and Public Freedom 69

35. Capitalist Attitudes: USA versus UK 71

36. The Concept of 'Needed Profit' 73

37. The Public Perception of Profit 74

38. The Profit Objective Fallacy 76

39. The Democratic Fallacy 78

40. Value Added: Use and Misuse 79

41. The Division of the Value Added between Capital and Labour 81

42. Value Added a Measure of Efficiency? 82

43. An Efficiency Improvement Target 84

44. The Timing of Renewals Expenditure 85

45. Investment: When? How Much? 89

46. How to Maximise your Pay 91

47. A Summary: Economics and Politics! 92

V **Starting Your Own Business** 94

48. A Case Study: Lyle Foods 94

49. Critical Factors 97

50. The Risk/Reward Matrix 100

51. Intelligence 103

52. A New Ally: the Internet 104

53. Research and Development 108

54. Choosing a Career 109

55. A Day in the Life of a Shift Manager 112

VI DIY Management 114

  56. Getting Started 114

  57. Priorities: 'Critical Areas' 116

  58. Using the Critical Areas' Concept 120

  59. Costing Products and By-Products 121

  60. Costing Export Products 124

  61. Basic Management Ploys 128

  62. Promoting 130

  63. Staff Development: Switching People 133

  64. Practical Leadership 135

  65. Paying Chairmen – and Others 139

  66. The Executive Pay Ratchet 143

  67. Managing Company Cars 145

  68. Managing Research 147

  69. Mechanisms for Innovation 149

  70. New Product Regulation 151

  71. A Siren's Voice: Diversification 153

  72. Size or Excellence? 154

Index 156

Preface

This book is not just about running a family business although that has its place. It aims to collect the ideas, concepts and some techniques of management for commercial and other organisations found by practical experience to work – and some not to work – in all sorts of situations. There are many people nowadays who find themselves managing something: a shop, an NHS hospital, a computer software business, a school, a law firm, a university, a museum or a sugar company. All share some common attributes, needs and language. I have tried to bring out practices that have a broad application and thus the book ranges between the most basic of managerial situations – simply getting a grip on a department one is expected suddenly to run – to topical issues like seniors' remuneration, the organisation of companies' boards of directors and a justification of the private enterprise system.

The thread binding these separate points together is for the most part their derivation from observing the operation of a commercial business run by strong people. Management history is made, like other histories, by individuals with ideas and power. Management essentially deals with flesh and blood. It has therefore seemed appropriate to leaven the dough by quoting stories about such people in real life situations, not all of them – I must admit – managerial ones. Work is to be enjoyed. We should not have that Monday morning feeling . . . in that spirit the reading in front of you is meant to be light. We should not take ourselves too seriously.

I have made much mention of members of my family. Regrettably some Tates have infiltrated themselves! You may call the firm Tate and Lyle. Many of us enjoyed it as Tate v. Lyle.

Introduction: the Family Business Background

Our experience shapes us. Much of mine was in a family-run company. Its managerial culture – and eccentricities – derive from its founders, owners and their characters. Some account of its origin and growth can illuminate our subject.

Henry Tate (later Sir Henry) started a grocery business in Lancashire in 1839 when he was twenty. He managed it well and could buy into a sugar refining partnership in 1859. It built a sugar refinery at Love Lane in Liverpool and one to make sugar cubes in Dockland London. Production grew and the cube trade – making large sparkling quick-dissolving cubes – became very profitable.

Abram Lyle had a shipping and sugar trading company in Greenock and became senior partner in a sugar refining company in1865 but he saw the future as lying with a big new refinery in London near to a large market. He sent his sons – one being my grandfather – to London to build and operate it. The enterprise was hazardous. The family had some £12 million in today's money tied up in sugar cargoes and a bank loan to finance construction. The bank panicked and demanded repayment. The most personable of the sons was sent to persuade it to the view that a completed factory might pay something while an aborted one could not. I banked for years with the Bank of Scotland. Once it sent my monthly statement in an unsealed envelope. I demanded privacy and received an instant apology – in an unsealed envelope (some disaffected post clerk?).

The refinery began work in 1883 and just survived. Wages were sometimes delayed. My grandfather at first could not afford half a penny for an evening paper. By 1900 Abram Lyle & Sons was very profitable, increasingly due to Lyle's Golden Syrup – a flavoursome richly-coloured spread of at that time unique consistency and quality.

But competition between the two families was severe and foreign imports further cut margins. The families never talked. The refinery directors going from their offices to the docks (in their frock coats and top hats) travelled in separate railway compartments. The Lyles were secretive. Disused plant was rendered unrecognisable with sledge hammers. Visitors were escorted in and out (and 100 years on the wheel has turned full circle). The Tates had professional managers to run the company. Their marketing policy was to supply customers with their wants even if the product range became lengthy. The Lyles themselves managed their business, deciding to concentrate on a few standard lines at minimum cost. By the Tuesday of each week they knew the profit and sugar loss for the preceding one!

In 1918 Ernest Tate (of whom it was said he could drink a bottle of Kummel a day) proposed a merger. There were varied motives. There was little profit on granulated sugar. With sugar a political football to compound the normal business risks, underwriting the long-term profitability of the mainline product appeared a paramount need. Furthermore, all but one of the Tate directors were retiring while the Lyles had two older and four younger men (one being my father) in the business. Succession and inheritance are serious matters in a family firm. For unclear reasons the negotiations dragged on for over two years. Though Tate had two refineries to our one and twice the production, their profit margin was half and the final terms were 50/50. Thus the formalities. Two cultures had to collaborate. For years two separate selling teams survived though large savings accrued from raw sugar purchasing (90% of a refiner's costs) and technical collaboration flourished. For once, the forecast merger benefits were actually realised.

When I joined the firm 27 years later the only survivors of the pre-merger battlefield were a robust good humour and an amicable rivalry. No Tate has married a Lyle, despite personal friendships. I was asked to give the Address at Johnny Tate's Memorial Service. Friendship can go no further.

Chapter I

A Family Business Management

'You can't help liking the managing director – if you don't,
he fires you.'

Anon

1 The Lyle Family Sugar Business

The part of Tate & Lyle I, aged 22 and just out of the Army, joined
in 1948 was the rump of a true family business. My great
grandfather, the third Abram Lyle, after running for some years a
shipping company and importing raw sugar from the West Indies,
became a partner in a Greenock sugar refinery. Fourteen years later
he decided the future lay with a new refinery close to a large market.
He sent his sons to London to build a factory on the River Thames
close to the Royal Docks, a place called Plaistow Wharf (pronounced
Plarstoe) and known to many East Enders. During its construction
the family fended off a threatened bank foreclosure. As Mr Anon
says, 'A banker . . . lends you an umbrella when the weather is fair,
and takes it away from you when it rains'. The refinery started
production in 1883. It had a precarious childhood: a chargehand I

1

knew told me his father had been asked like all employees to take a wage cut one year. We achieved financial resilience around 1910, by then making in the year 120,000 tons of white sugar and 21,000 tons of Lyle's Golden Syrup (in the local patois, Goldie). When my training commenced the sugar output was 400,000 tons, with 41,000 tons of Goldie.

Basic wages were a *constant* 24 shillings a week from 1895 to 1912, the country's rising income per head and companies' increasing productivity appearing as falling prices – the inversion of post-war Britain. In 1903 40 cigarettes cost 11 ½ pence and a pint of real beer 2 ½ pence. One of our employees, Herbert Woodward, who started work in that year, used to have 'a good evening' out for a shilling.

A core of skilled staff had come down from Greenock with the family, almost as big a decision as emigrating for an ordinary person without a nest egg. I got to know a number of their descendants. A tradition of long service was built up. The Lyles controlled and managed the company but nepotism, I'm selfishly pleased to say, spread from top to bottom. When I joined, 47% of Plaistow's 2500 employees had relations in T & L.

For years competition was very severe in sugar and Lyle's depended on Goldie for much of its profit. In 1921 older members of each family proposed an amalgamation with Tate's. Philip and Oliver Lyle, my father and uncle, were opposed to the merger, fearing loss of freedom and the constraints of being a sizeable public company. They were far-sighted. Until my generation the families maintained a privileged position but declining shareholdings in a growing public company meant the day of the professional manager was arriving. The moral is clear. If you want to keep your company as your own business with opportunities for your family and an inheritance for them, you must eschew going public – or at least keep the company modestly sized and highly profitable. Short-term benefits in terms of growth and revenues and diversification may look enticing. In the long run you will lose your company through them.

2 A Little Background: Sugar Refining

Sugar cane is a grass – big, but to the botanist still a grass. Its cultivation exposes management issues as we shall see later. After 12 to 18 months' growth the cane is ripe and it is cut, transported by cart or truck or wagon to the local raw sugar factory where the sugar is squeezed out of the fibre in a massive multi-roller mill – its drive consumes around 1500 horsepower – purified and crystallised into a sticky solid, raw sugar, the earliest processing stage to yield a stable, transportable product able to stand long storage in ship or silo before final purification in a 'refinery'.

At the factory non-sugar impurities not finding their way into the raw and not into products like Demerara sugar for local consumption, are rejected but – being sticky – take a little sugar with them – hence 'cane molasses'. The fibre is dried and burned in the boilers, a free fuel. Plain dirt – press mud – returns to the land as fertiliser. The

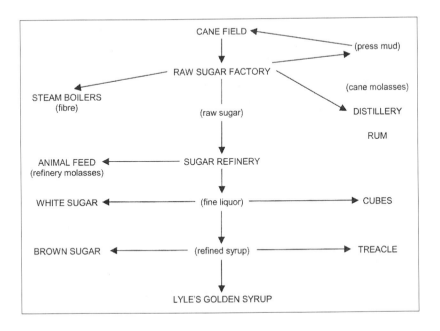

remaining impurities in the raw sugar end up in 'refinery molasses' or in brown sugars, syrups and treacles.

It has often been asked, 'why a separate refinery?' Why not complete the whole process in a combined operation under one roof and one management? This could be advantageous technically as well as increasing the proportion of added value retained in the often poor cane growing country. Practical difficulties undermine theory. A refinery may draw raws from many countries – West Indies, Hawaii, Australia, South Africa, or home grown beet sugar – so is not a seasonal operation; a raw factory works only for three months during harvest. A refinery five or ten times as big and working all year can be cheaper. Being often sited in a temperate climate it can more easily recruit skilled and expert staff to improve its efficiency. Most decisively, a refinery is physically close to its customers: their needs can be met promptly with minimum stocks by a 'just-in-time' system; package material, a very costly item, need only stand a truck journey to a retailer's warehouse, not an ocean crossing in the probably dirty hold of a 50,000 ton cargo boat or bulk carrier.

Is beet sugar as sweet as cane? Yes, it is. Can one tell the difference? A skilled chemist can discover the sugar's origin by analysing its impurities. Don't bees distinguish between beet and cane? Trace impurities used to give them diarrhoea; though refined beet sugar is now very pure, a trace may have the same effect.

Do companies own factories and refineries? Some do. T & L used to have three factories in the West Indies; their staff were staggered to discover that their entire season's production kept Plaistow going for under ten weeks. We later shed them. I think tactical reasons may justify such ownership but it may well be a strategic error unless the two operations are geographically and physically separate, as are T & L's current investments in Hungary and Australia. Vertical integration may well reduce efficiency: you may feel impelled to accept the factory's output at its cost – and anyhow, what should that be? Local politics may complicate life for a big company: it is

4

liable to become saddled with social obligations and pressed for short-term opportunism. These arguments are general ones and apply outside the sugar industry.

Surely molasses is good for you? It may be. The minerals and trace elements in it may help if the diet is deficient – though accurate guidance on that is hard to find. Molasses may well be good for the bowels but it, especially beet molasses, has a bitter taste – it's only 50% sugar. T & L felt unable to supply it for the domestic market because its quality in terms of cleanliness and consistency could not be guaranteed. Its treacles and syrups to a degree could match the possible benefits without sacrifice of quality.

3 Managing Cane Cultivation

A cane sugar factory typically produces 130,000 tonnes of raw sugar per year from around a million tonnes of cane, working for three months or so, to get the ripe crop off before the rainy season arrives when the cane will spoil and transport is difficult. To do this it works flat out, with a conventional emphasis on throughput over efficiency – a questionable choice. While fuel – fibre from the cane – is free, sugar is not. Good extraction can be everything.

For every 100 tonnes of sugar in the cane coming from the field some three-quarters reaches a ship for moving to big consumer countries while the rest disappears in the cheap molasses or down the drain. If, then, the factory extraction can be screwed up from 75 to 76% – surely a trivial improvement? – 47,000 tonnes less cane need be planted, weeded, cut, transported and milled for the same sales, freeing some 1200 acres of land in the process. Not so trivial. Hence the adage, money is made in the field and lost in the factory. It's an example of identifying which aspect of business performance exerts real leverage.

Performance deserves measuring. Field cultivation costs are largely proportional to area, not to yield of cane per acre. It pays heartily therefore to increase this yield: the marginal profit is high. The longer the growth period the less intensive the harvesting and anyway we want sugar, not cane for its own sake, so the measure of agricultural performance becomes tonnes of sugar delivered to the factory per acre per year.

What makes for good cultivation? Interestingly, it's not best done in low-lying tropical countries. Sun and soil make cane stalks expand but not necessarily filling the interstices with sugar. Night-time cold – for example a touch of frost in high lands like Zambia – checks physical extension and the energy goes into creating sugar instead.

Cane is mostly grown on big estates, say of 30,000 acres, staffed with agronomists and engineers, all managed in modern systems and much science. Alongside the estate a native farmer grows a few tonnes on his small patch – as cheaply or cheaper than the big producer: his overhead is trivial, his cultivation intensive, his motivation clear and he has his own enterprise. There is a lesson in this.

Around 1950 raw sugar began to be shipped loose in the ships' holds, and instead of in bags. To smooth the transition a colleague, John Ellyatt, was sent to the port of Rotterdam to examine its methods. He met a Frenchman on an identical assignment but who was busy trying to get it off with a local girl. On the eve of his departure victory looked assured: he was in bed in her flat next to the railway line. At the crucial moment with a sudden ferocious roar, an express train howled past. The girl (somehow) sat up in bed, 'Ah, monsieur, the 10.15 from Lille!'

4 Is Your Product Unhealthy?

Like most companies supplying consumer products sugar refiners have been attacked for profiting from unhealthiness. To counter such attitudes calls first for facts to be established.

In our case the criticisms were simple. 'Refining removes the goodness'. 'Refined sugar is bad for you'. 'Sugar is empty calories'. Let us see if it is. Typical raw sugar entering a refinery contains 0.45% of mineral matter, 0.62% organic matter and 0.56% of invert sugar; all the rest is in the chemist's term sucrose, the sugar you buy in the shop. Invert has no more or no less nutritional value than sucrose; chemically they are almost identical. But invert is metabolised more slowly which may suit some people, especially diabetics. T & L did not offer it because it is expensive to crystallise and hygroscopic (picks up moisture) and it is that form which is convenient and has a long shelf life. Organic matter is largely proteins and amino acids: if it is a nutrient the quantity is tiny. There are far better sources of protein. The minerals could well be useful, especially if trace elements which regulate the body's metabolism are included – but raws vary and such elements are ill-understood. So there *may* be up to 1.07% of valuable material lost to white sugar. Domestic consumption is circa 30 lb per head per year so we are talking about losing under half a gram a day. Vegetables are a preferable source. In any case, if you do want our source you can buy brown sugars and syrups. As only 5% of sales take this form the pundits – who really only seem paradoxically happy with dirty foods from surgically clean factories – are being ignored.

To counter these arguments we joined with other British sugar companies in running an information bureau to brief the press and other interested parties and to provide literature and teaching aids to schools. Although known to be a perhaps biased source it has proved beneficial. Its clients are sensible. A source of information may be biased. That means you *may* need to check it. It does *not* mean its argument can be ignored. However biased persons may be their arguments have to be in logic refuted or accepted.

There has also been a more positive attack: 'white sugar is bad for you'. The attackers have not all been very respectable. Fashions in favoured diets change. After so many shifting positions the public is becoming sceptical. (How's this for commonsense? 'Food is an important part of a balanced diet' – Fran Lebowitz). But it is still our duty to know our subject.

For nearly forty years T & L has been a member of the World Sugar Research Organisation (WSRO) and for much of that time I was fortunate to be our representative on its Board. Its role is to monitor, encourage, finance and co-ordinate health research world-wide. We thus kept in touch with all opinion on and investigation of our product. Modem comprehensive well designed studies – i.e. those allowing for peoples' differing genetic make-up, constitutions, dietary and other habits, and environments – disclose no statistically significant connection between sugar consumption and all the diseases it has been accused of fostering, with the exception of dental caries. Fortunately the latter in this fluoride era is of much decreasing importance.

This is a thoroughly dull conclusion for the media and a knock – which they fail to perceive – for 'experts' lecturing us on all that is bad for us. Moderation in all things seems the only safe conclusion in the present state of dietary expertise. Even this humble conclusion may be a matter of opinion. Bernard Levin in *The Times* gave a splendid example of robust scepticism about my (and others') views, which he introduced thus: 'Enough of these niminy-piminy folk. I'll take my stand on that great man Wing Commander Paddy Barthrop . . . I took him to dinner once, and he described (as he ate) his idea of good eating. It went like this:

I eat everything, as much butter and fried foods as I can get my hands on. My favourite meal is roast lamb with onion sauce, thick with cream, and spuds with butter on. I smoke between 40 and 60 cigarettes a day. To eat cornflakes you've got to have sugar on them, and lots of cream, otherwise there is no point in eating them. I am purely a social drinker . . . if there's a party I drink as much whisky and water as I can get my hands on, no ice, and as much wine as they are prepared to buy me. The older you get the less booze you can take, which must be good for your liver. Now, after a few large whiskies and a bottle of vino, I'm gone. I have a main meal at night. I'm very fond of haggis with mashed potatoes with bags of cream and a dollop of butter. I like all food – smoked salmon, lobsters, as long as you keep smoking cigarettes, drinking plenty of whisky and tap water – not this rubbish in a bottle – you'll go on for ever.

As quite often happens membership of the WSRO had a useful and unexpected by-product as well as equipping us to cope with product safety concerns. Its meetings attracted the senior people from sugar companies all over the world. In a relaxed open situation we could discuss matters of mutual interest and be exposed to other countries' thinking – a useful antidote to parochialism.

5 Lyle's Golden Syrup: Quality Control

The family company prospered over the years. Then called Abram Lyle & Sons, it was highly geared so moderate profits yielded a high return on the family equity holding. For a time the directors received a dividend of 2% a fortnight with a final of 50% at Christmas! This reflected no more than a tolerable profit on a very modest capital base.

Severe competition, particularly with Tate's refineries, constrained sugar profit; with Goldie the family had found a valuable niche product. Without it survival would have been tested. Syrup making began early and quality, personally controlled by the refinery directors, was steadily improved. Its profitability and their own high standards demanded their personal attention. The trade mark on the cans – Samson's lion with its quotation from Judges XIV – became well known. In December 1979 I received this letter:

Dear Sir,
Why do you have a lion with wasps all around it on your syrup tin.
When I have breakfast I all ways [sic] wonder why. Please can you tell
me.

From
Justin Sims (age 7)

I enjoyed replying. The lively story of Samson bears retelling. He, an
Israelite, was attracted to a Philistine woman in Timnath and told
his parents he would wed her. They preferred an Israelite girl for him;
they didn't know that with the Lord's encouragement he sought a
casus belli with the Philistines who then controlled Israel:

Then went Samson down, and his father and his mother, to Timnath,
and came to the vineyards of Timnath: and, behold, a young lion
roared against him. And the spirit of the Lord came mightily upon
him, and he rent him as he would have rent a kid, and he had nothing
in his hand . . . And he went down, and talked with the woman; and
she pleased Samson well. And after a time he returned to take her and
he turned aside to see the carcase of the lion: and, behold, there was a
swarm of bees and honey in the carcase . . . So his father went down
unto the woman: and Samson made there a feast; for so used the
young men to do. And it came to pass, when they saw him, that they
brought thirty companions to be with him. And Samson said unto
them, I will now put forth a riddle unto you: if ye can certainly declare
it me within the seven days of the feast, and find it out, then I will give
you thirty sheets and thirty changes of garments: But if ye cannot
declare it me, then shall ye give me thirty sheets and thirty changes of
garments. And they said unto him, Put forth thy riddle, that we may
hear it. And he said unto them, Out of the eater came forth meat, and
out of the strong came forth sweetness. And they could not in three
days expound the riddle. And it came to pass on the seventh day, that
they said unto Samson's wife, Entice thy husband, that he may declare
unto us the riddle, lest we burn thee and thy father's house with fire. .
And Samson's wife wept before him, and said, Thou dost but hate me,

10

and lovest me not: thou has put forth a riddle unto the children of my people, and hast not told it me . . . and it came to pass on the seventh day, that he told her, because she lay sore upon him: and she told the riddle to the children of her people. And the men of the city said unto him . . . What is sweeter than honey? and what is stronger than a lion? And he said unto them, If ye had not plowed with my heifer, ye had not found out my riddle. And the Spirit of the Lord came upon him, and he went down to Ashkelon, and slew thirty men of them, and took their spoil, and gave change of garments unto them which expounded the riddle. And his anger was kindled, and he went up to his father's house. But Samson's wife was given to his companion, whom he had used as his friend.

Samson's subsequent career was equally violent. After a time he visited his wife but her father forbade him entry. Samson therefore burned Philistine fields and vineyards. Angered, the Philistines burned his wife and her father. Samson promised revenge: 'he smote them hip and thigh with a great slaughter', before retiring to seclusion. Three thousand men of Judah then delivered him bound to the Philistines but he burst his bonds and killed a thousand of them with the jaw-bone of an ass. Another ambush when Samson was visiting a harlot in Gaza failed but now his time was come: he met Delilah.

Goldie manufacture was naturally shrouded in obsessive secrecy. As a boy Oliver Lyle was as a privilege shown the very effective method of thickening the syrup: 'That is how we do it and you must never never tell this to anyone'.

Syrup is heavy, 1.4 times as heavy as water, and a cheap but strong pack for it was a lever lid steel can. The directors had always interested themselves in the Can Making Department and managed it with the foreman, by-passing the managerial organisation. This broke all the rules, caused little irritation and worked: productivity increased tenfold in eighteen years. The combination of inventive interested leaders – Oliver and the foreman and the chief fitter – with time to study and think and with the power to implement their ideas explains this.

The by-passing too can be explained. The morale when I was a very junior trainee was so patently high that no one feared trespassers. Job descriptions were sparse or purely verbal traditions so overlaps resulted. As long as all necessary work was done no one worried about who did what. The absence of company politics and inter-departmental jealousies was very marked and wholly refreshing. It shows that neither is inevitable.

Refinery directors' concerns extended beyond dabbling in can making: quality and taste were closely watched. They tasted a sample almost daily – as I did in my time. No change in process technique was permitted without their sanction – which was rarely forthcoming. The staff were well aware of this and of the emphasis on quality. The process worker mixed each tankful – it was in part a batch process – and the lab technician checked the analysis; both well knew even at their level that they would not be criticised at all if they rejected a batch not quite up to standard but would be upbraided if they let it pass in the interests of a quiet life. The decision rules were clear.

The outcome was that you were more likely to be dealt a royal flush at poker than you were to buy a faulty can of syrup. In this quality conscious age certain messages are obvious.

6 Family Management

From its earliest days the Lyles managed the business closely; they had between them sufficient talent – or believed they had – to dispense with imported professional managers at the top. Tate did not and while the talent sufficed the Lyles had an advantage: hands on management by a motivated close-knit group made for decisive and speedy action. And prior to my generation there was the talent. For years the Plaistow directors were Philip and Oliver Lyle. Philip knew his mathematics, engineering and chemistry; Oliver was an electrical engineer who also knew his thermodynamics and chemical engineering technology ('The worst misfortune that can happen to an ordinary man is to have an extraordinary father' – Austen O'Malley). Thus equipped they could and did dominate their technical staff; they knew enough to judge technical, financial or safety arguments for themselves. They could not be bamboozled with science (although the later staff were highly qualified, I believe directors should have enough knowledge to assess expenditure or technical changes for themselves: the adage, 'the managing director is the board member who knows where the factory is', is not too safe).

The refinery directors, being both creative, could introduce new ideas and implement them. I was going to say, against all opposition, but their power and intellectual standing demolished this, such as it was. Being a twosome – against all management theory – conferred authority. They could discuss very fully managerial matters between themselves before consulting their managers so there was none of the loneliness of the long distance boss and there was freedom from time-wasting debate. Being brothers there was no power politics. It was a system which was perpetuated into the late sixties and worked as well with a pair made up of a family man and non-family man as with relations.

In those spacious times directors could travel for their health or to learn what other factories were doing. While touring a Hungarian beet factory Oliver missed seeing a syrup tank with its brim flush with the floor (if there had been a factory inspectorate someone would have been shot). Oliver stepped back – into the tank. Fortunately it was neither hot nor mechanically stirred; his hosts fished him out and his suit cooled off and crystallised solid, forming a huge mobile lollipop. A late-comer, my cousin Ian Lyle, a man of singular character and intellect, joined Oliver at Plaistow. Together they toured American can making plants and were met by a lively gentleman named Mr Euphrat – 'EUPHRAT, same as the River Euphrat'. The war with Hitler called Ian to serve in motor torpedo boats, based at Newhaven. Enjoying his drink, expeditions to London were lively affairs. Returning full of port late at night he insisted on driving the train – against no great resistance – from Lewes to Newhaven. British Rail might like to offer this as a perk to loyal customers.

In the 1939–45 War Oliver managed the refinery by himself. Staff and equipment shortages, air raids – the nearby docks were an attractive target – and rationing made for technical demoralisation and high costs per unit but not for low morale. Everyone knew the brass were as exposed to bombing as were process workers; in this respect like an admiral who lives as dangerously in a battle as an ordinary seaman. All served in the local Home Guard (Dad's Army) and on fire-watching duty. To help women working awkward hours on shift, the company paid for a Bond Street hairdresser to attend regularly. She used to find lice for which Oliver made apologetic noises. She crisply replied, 'Forget it – plenty of lice in Bond Street.'

Many of our managers had gone to the war, to absorb in demanding conditions managerial lessons – on leadership, care of your men, personal development, communications, problem-solving. A version of the latter confronted our transport manager, 'Nibs' Hiscocks. The Army recognised his knowledge. He was ordered one day to drive General de Gaulle to meet Churchill at Chequers. He was given a driver and car and they collected the great man but no directions. Nobody knew the way and for security reasons signposts were lacking. For reasons I can't recollect it took three days to deliver the cargo. Nibs expected to be beheaded on Tower Hill. Churchill took him aside, 'Any officer who can lose General de Gaulle for three days stands high in my estimation'.

Philip, Oliver and Ian exemplify a strong innovative management running their own business with the time, authority and imagination to explore constantly ways of improving it and to get these

14

implemented, while maintaining a personal relationship with their able staff and their mostly very loyal workers. Against this must be set the production orientation. We weren't market-lead. Over the years Goldie's quality was improved, interpreted as reducing its colour and non-sugar content. What the public wanted was not then asked. A loss of flavour was the danger signal – and was belatedly recognised. It was left to competitors to offer more flavoured and coloured products like treacle. As a boy I asked my father if Tate made a golden syrup. He replied, 'Well, they call it syrup but it's gear oil really'. This production cast of mind was not inevitable. All it needed was a powerful preferably family man as Marketing Director. Later a Sales Director appeared, Charles Lyle, whose activity was circumscribed by a marked passivity (he had circumnavigated the recruitment system). Philip and Oliver used to creep up to his office and open the door suddenly to catch him hastily snatching a document from his desk drawer to show he had been working. In this important endeavour they usually triumphed. Of course the family ruled in more easy-going times so they could readily avoid one modern failing: younger managers sacking older staff for a short-term pay-off:

> The result is that a number of companies now find themselves devoid of experience and intellect and in the hands of 'dynamic' but implausible second-class management . . . I know of no other country where experience is discarded so lightly. 'This approach,' goes on Mr Chris Stiles in *The Times* of March 1994, 'influences recruitment: One sees all too frequently the "macho" qualities . . . highlighted by words like "dynamic", "aggressive" . . . "high calibre" . . . Of course anyone aspiring to a role in senior management needs to bring energy and enthusiasm to the task, but where is the emphasis on the cerebral qualities needed to run a company – the ability to think things through, an analytical, problem-solving mind, perseverance, patience, wide experience, integrity? These do not appear high on a recruiter's list.'

7 Family Recruitment

When the company was a frail youth it could carry only a few top executives. The Lyles rationed themselves to one son each to be eligible for entry, as a way of deciding who was to be offered a chance and who not. Philip entered by this rule but younger brother Oliver could not. However, one of the previous generation eloped with an attractive woman from the Packeting Department and was frozen out by a stern family; this vacancy Oliver filled. She deserved well of the republic.

In my time T & L was a large public company with many outside shareholders who expected an emphasis on competence – fortunately for me not to excess. Normally Tate or Lyle relatives had no promise of a job but this could follow if they took the opportunity to prove their worth. This they could do by training to be a Shift Manager in a refinery, that is, being responsible for almost the entire factory's production and people for an eight-hour shift. The non-family intake, often university graduates, joined the same stream and for an equivalent assessment of their qualities. Though shift working was personally tiresome the job was extremely satisfying: within a mere fourteen months of starting one could have a highly responsible position which incidentally gave an insight into the entire refinery management – making for enhanced personal development.

There was a discreet surveillance and reporting system operated by one's boss, the Process Manager, with trusted foremen, of which one was unconscious. Informal feedback was the input to appraisal and seemed to work reliably. If one passed, fine; if not, out. It was colloquially known as the Shit or Bust System (S or B in the vernacular). For the surviving family men there followed a period on shift, before rotation round the whole business to learn commercial, financial, costing, selling and similar activities. Apart from acquiring knowledge one obtained an insight into informal company affairs and met all sorts of employees. If one was clean about the house and eager to learn one's reception was warm. Any arrogance was soon reported and for one family person I knew it earned instant dismissal.

This was the normal but not the sole procedure. For example, 'Long John' Tate was brought in for his mathematical ability and character, not for his managerial strength then unrecognised. There was a story, no doubt apocryphal, that Peter Runge, a senior director, had personally recruited him from Cambridge because of his alleged insistence on keeping a woman in his room at college. He short-circuited the normal induction process and was given special assignments to tap his analytical ability – to the company's benefit.

The recruitment process was thus sensibly flexible: it could employ horses for courses. The main entry stream through the Shift Manager circuit for S or Bs was operated with some severity, a highly necessary condition for nepotism to be acceptable or at least tolerated.

This is the likely scenario for a family business. Its founders may well want to hand on a legacy as well as give themselves congenial employment. The recruitment and training arrangements must therefore be thought through. Anyone joining an overtly family company must and will expect young sprigs to join. However, without certain standards of competence applying to them there will be anger in other staff and risk to the company's survival. If the latter is in question recruiting a marginal person is doing him and everyone else no favours. The able family person's promotion after induction deserves separate discussion.

8 Family Promotion

Speedy elevation to the peerage rather than accelerated promotion was part of the S or B system. If you were an S, this meant being thought to be of potentially Board material but with this S label one fears Mr Anon's comment: 'You're the sort of person Dr Spooner would have called a shining wit!'. After a mere six years or so, spent learning what the company did and how it did it and who was who, as well as being given ad hoc projects and jobs to perform, you could find yourself called a director.

The theory behind this Canaveral-like launch was that you would not clutter up intermediate levels of management, to which everyone else could aspire; you would only occupy the few top jobs at which very few could realistically aim anyway in a family business. The practice could work as designed in earlier times but modernity, the degradation of family financial control and the rather average level of in-coming family talent all undermined respect for it. (I'm very glad that the whole anachronistic system saw out my time.)

While one learned much about the company – in my case much about production and sugar technology – the theory of management went ignored. Those who had attempted formulating it were deemed impracticable. Practical working was the thing. The fact that in logic theory must precede practice was unacceptable. Young sprigs found themselves in senior positions with no conceptual scheme of thought to guide them. The categorisation of managerial work into planning, organising, leading and controlling – which was still a rather simple but nonetheless a helpful start – came to one's attention later.

Inevitably one floundered. I was not wholly unprepared. I volunteered for the Army at age eighteen and joined up in 1944. Eighteen months as a private was instructive: life consisted of grappling daily with a stream of stupid orders raining down on one from unreasonable men – not, I fear, much different from many a civilian shop floor. A couple of years as a senior NCO taught me little. It should have done more. As orderly sergeant I had to inspect the food in the canteens and hear complaints. As a Shift Manager I took my supper at 2 am. in a corner of the works canteen with the duty customs officer and the senior foreman while my shift were eating; to my shame I hardly ever inspected the meals, nor I think did colleagues. The services would have jumped on such neglect.

Nowadays I suspect they are much better at training; the Army has for long been good at man management, much better in fact than industry. A bit of looking over the fence to observe one's neighbour's methods of husbandry wouldn't go amiss. A relevant practice is the moving of officers through a succession of postings, with or without promotion. I think a couple of years too short to master an industrial role but industry errs in the other direction: managers are left for many years in the same job. It should be a drill to review length of tenure.

The S or B system could still be applicable to a modern family business, but modified. The initial training should be much broader than mine. Pre-job experience could be beneficial. I don't think it much matters what. It could be managing a garage in France or VSO or bicycling across Russia or cleaning aircraft at Heathrow or joining the Royal Navy. None of these would be wasted time. A Sabbatical during or after training could increase knowledge, give outside experience and freshen up a person before promotion. On re-entry, perhaps having won his spurs in terms of knowledge or success, the prodigal son could appear more acceptable, usefully experienced and worthy of some notice. Demonstrating competence in the anointed deserves close attention; after all, King Edward III at the Battle of Crecy in 1346 risked defeat by setting up his son, the Black Prince, in a decisive role for the English army. These devices could make the recruitment and promotion arrangements respectable while still meeting the founders' objectives of providing congenial employment for the next generation. It could have a valuable by-product. Most such recruits may well be not that extraordinary but a minority will be Young Turks. How else do you find and insert such creatures into positions of influence while they are still young and inspired?

Some of these points apply to selecting and promoting graduates or similar animals, whether family or not. I don't believe three years at university studying – in moderation – classics or history ill fits a person from joining a technical industry. I think a First may indicate a good exam passer, not necessarily a broadly educated wise mature person. And someone with a short service commission in the Army behind him or her may well surpass the Oxbridge graduate as interesting material. Finally, beware rejecting or passing over older people. Age equates with experience; having solved a problem before makes for effortlessness next time.

Chris Stiles told this horror story in *The Times*:

I have a friend who has spent the last ten years running two successful ... companies, the first in the UK, the second in America. He returned to the UK, at the age of 51, and sought a similar chief executive role. After a frustrating year of interviews but no offers, he had to settle for involvement with a consulting group specialised in his industry. He was surprised to find that four or five companies which he had approached ... which had rejected him in favour of other applicants, were now on his list of clients. Without exception he was appalled at the modest capability of the people who had been preferred to him. Their management mistakes were predictable and avoidable, and their business acumen sadly lacking: their way of overcoming the mess which they inevitably created was to hire management consultants ... Had [my friend] been a recruiter for any of the companies involved, he would not have hired any of them.

Chapter II

Technologies to Improve a Business

'My computer dating bureau came up with a perfect
gentleman. Still, I've got another three goes.'

– *Sally Poplin*

9 Packeting Productivity in Town and Country

Granulated sugar was conveniently packed in 2 lb (now 1 kg) paper
bags, 14 of which (or similar multiple of 1 kg bags) are wrapped in
kraft paper parcels and loaded onto a pallet to form a mechanically
handled 1 tonne lot. The arrangement allowed us to pack more
cheaply than the grocer, an option which was always open to him.
For years we had used packeting machines made by Hesser of
Stuttgart and were big customers of theirs. Philip Lyle negotiated the
first order in 1927 and thirty-eight years later I visited Hesser. The
Sales Manager had been at that first meeting, which was conducted
in German as my father spoke it fluently. While negotiating, he and
his director had wanted a private word and switched from German
to the Swabian dialect. My father had interrupted their talk: 'You
ought to know, gentlemen, that I also know the Swabian dialect'.

21

The Hessers at Plaistow worked at about 80–85% efficiency, when 100% would have been achieved if the actual output was the theoretical machine speed (66 packets per minute) times the nominal working hours in an 8 hour day less meal breaks. A local labour shortage in the East End made us build a packeting station at Keynsham near Bristol with 10 Hessers fed by loose sugar in bulk tankers from London. Its efficiency – that is the actual output of nicely packed sugar relative to the theoretically possible amount in working hours – was consistently 96% or better and sometimes over 100% – this with identical machines identically installed and manned. We ascribed this remarkable performance to a combination of factors:

- The Keynsham people were virtually country folk, not from a city.

- The department was small and physically compact – about 60 people in all.

- The manager, an ex-Plaistovian, was very good and supported by pleasant able craftsmen.

- There perhaps was some 'Hawthorne effect',* seniors from Plaistow visited the station regularly and of course attended social events.

The explanation of the 101% was that the women sometimes quite voluntarily cut short their meal breaks and set their machines going again; perhaps they got bored hanging around after a meal. They didn't look bored. Thus there seemed to us no magic about the overall performance of the station: it was the natural consequence of

---

*Westinghouse's Hawthorne plant saw a work-study of one department. The lighting, machine layout and so on were improved. At each change productivity improved. Some genius ordered all to revert to the original. Output went up. It was ascribed to the girls enjoying unwonted interest and attention from people clearly concerned with their needs.

good management and smallness away from the big city. We ought to have anticipated this benefit. For the Ideal Home Exhibition at Olympia some years previously we had set up a Hesser on a stand and worked it continuously to intrigue a stream of viewers. The women operating it were from Plaistow, the machine was very reliable and the efficiencies very high; they must have enjoyed being on show and having an appreciative audience – the Hawthorne effect with a vengeance.

The Hesser worked at 3960 packets per hour. A British machine came along with twice the speed. This at first glance looked highly attractive. But deciding the optimum rate is an interesting business. I suggest faster may well not be cheaper – or better. While a packeting machine is working the only cost it is incurring is the interest on its capital cost. When it stops it incurs extra costs: labour to clear a jammed bag or to clean up a spillage, a fitter to mend something, more package material to replace what has been damaged, and so on. The machine should work slowly enough to avoid stoppages. As we have seen the old Hesser was very good at this.

A Hesser had a multitude of grease points and servicing was done every ten days and took several hours per machine. One day I thought to query this with the foreman engineer: what could he suggest? He made an immediate response. Several things could be done: guarding bearings from loose sugar and suchlike. I offered the idea of changing the grease to molybdenum disulphide, just then becoming recommended by Rolls-Royce for its cars. I said, 'Extend the servicing intervals as much as you dare; if anything breaks I'll take the responsibility. All right?' He went to work with enthusiasm. Within a matter of weeks the servicing interval was extended from every ten days to every ten weeks. It only needed a modest stimulus to tap the resident talent.

At that time the Weights and Measures Act demanded very few underweight packets and limited overweights. To conform we checked samples regularly from our weighing machines on special scales to an accuracy of 0.04%. The cost of scales and full-time checkers was substantial and served only to make each packet identical. As a household bought say twenty packets a year a more flexible law without checkweighing, relying on weighing errors being random – we didn't volume fill which can develop a bias – would have given the buyer the same weight of sugar per year at less cost. But I'm sure such elasticity would not have found political favour.

10 Production Scheduling

Sugar refining is a series of standard chemical engineering processes – solid/liquid centrifugal separation, filtration, crystallisation, and so on, in outline simple, in detail complex. Sugar liquors deteriorate in heat so inter-process storage must be minimised unless batch processes are to become starved and kept idle. Plant sizing, automated flow control, the refinery load factor – all can be combined for the optimum balance. Raw and refined stocks come into the equation. For years we did not apply top management's attention to the subject. Increasing automaticity and computerised control have forced the issue.

Prodded by very able management consultants, we set up an Operations Department headed by an ex-refinery manager, a senior man – five people in all. Its role was to optimise production and packing of all refineries on a weekly basis by balancing supplies against demand by area and by refinery in the light of local constraints and potential . It very quickly earned its keep.

A sugar refinery is partly at the mercy of its input raw sugars. Natal raws used to be notoriously difficult to filter and output could sag by a third or more – a vastly expensive matter. Like T & L's other refineries Plaistow had two or three staff people – not in but alongside line production – to help solve such technical problems. They were older, had long experience and were stuffed with refining lore and principles. They had seen it all before. When not problem-solving they were conducting experiments or taking out heat balances or specifying new plant. Their overall contribution was worth far more than their salaries. I fear that they have been made redundant to save short-term costs.

I suspect these lessons apply outside the sugar business. The first is, production scheduling may be a bore but needs attention by someone. Now 'just-in-time' is the watchword and logistics are managed with care. The second is that a factory rids itself – in the name of productivity – of 'old sweats' who can deal with production hazards and improvements at its peril.

11 How to Halve Fuel Consumption

A sugar refinery uses, or ought to use, about 1 tonne of steam and 50 to 100 kwh of electricity per tonne of sugar. On the fifties' prices a 1% saving in steam was equivalent just at marginal cost to saving 1 ½ men – quite big money. Aware of the scope to improve usage Philip and Oliver initiated a major economy campaign in the thirties. Over some five years they *halved* coal consumption per tonne of sugar; some third of the saving arose from renewing a process, another third from new boilers and turbines and the balance with little capital expenditure from heat saving devices where cost savings went almost straight through to the bottom line. The methods were quite simple:

Installing steam meters to see who used what and to show the users what they were using.

Re-using heat: for example, if you boil a liquid you can use the vapour coming off to heat your central heating system for free.

Reducing processing temperatures – and reducing sugar loss as a by-product.

25

Stopping gland leaks, saving flash from steam traps, etc.

Lagging hot pipes and tanks.

Of these techniques I think the re-use of heat is the most elegant. Some of Plaistow's heat was used four times before rejection as too low grade to be useful. Power saving is more difficult, in fact steam saving may increase its consumption, but a refinery can generate steam at high pressure and pass it through a turbo-alternator, thus generating the power it needs and exhausting the steam at low pressure for process use. The resulting power is much cheaper than grid power. This 'Combined Heat and Power' system (CHP) can show an overall efficiency of some 75% compared with the 40% or so in the best power stations.

The lessons are these. Steam saving is not difficult – the techniques are very well established – and boosts the bottom line very nicely; both company and country are beneficiaries from CHP; the matter deserves management's personal attention. Astonishingly, there are companies operating today without even lagging hot pipes. How to let money float away on the air.

To expand on the last point, management attention. Philip and Oliver had the time for the work, being free of routine duties: they had a General Manager, also a Lyle, to run the refinery for them. They also had the motive, being large shareholders, and the knowledge – both knew more than enough physics and sugar technology to lead the campaign. They also had a full-time technologist, free of all routine, to devil for them.

Plaistow made a large investment in two high pressure boilers, back pressure turbines and much associated equipment. The boilers were fed with water under pressure, each with its own supply pumps which were duplicated for security of supply; there was an inter-connecting pipe, normally shut, in case one supply failed and the other was needed – no water and the boiler tubes are destroyed. Oliver was in the Boiler House when one feed pump failed. The standby should have tripped in automatically. It didn't. The foreman spotted the rapidly approaching crisis and leaped down the stairs to get at the valve on the inter-connecting pipe. Oliver watched and followed him.. He rushed down the stairs and flung himself on the huge valve and with a monstrous effort managed to open it. Crisis over. Next day two men with crowbars couldn't shift the valve. With so much equipment the refinery was almost a power station. Today fuel technology and pricing slants the balance: it pays to install the largest turbine you can use and sell the resulting surplus power to the grid, making good money while you do it. The return on the investment can be so high that it pays to renew a power plant even if it is quite young.

As a young trainee Oliver had been in on the test of Plaistow's first turbine in 1912. To show off, as he told me, he brashly ordered the governor controlling the steam supply (and thus the turbine speed) to be tested. It failed, and the turbine promptly ran away, '. . . to nearly twice full speed with a noise like a diabolically dignified siren', as it went through various critical speeds when it was out of balance. Everyone took to their heels except for Oliver, who daren't as he'd ordered the test, and a young fitter who calmly and without fuss walked over and shut the steam supply valve. Oliver could remember the feel of an unbalanced turbine for long after. Much later I felt it when facing a crash shutdown in the middle of the night due to a boiler breakdown – as the steam supply failed the turbine lost speed and shook till its lagging fell off. It scared me. Much later still I was in a Pan Am 747 over Greenland when I felt a familiar vibration; I wasn't surprised when the captain told us he'd had to shut down a jet engine for lack of oil pressure.

12 Computer Hazards

T & L joined the computing fraternity early, if not in the stone age then in the iron age. When I became responsible for the department we had an IBM 1401 with a miserable 8K of core storage! It was a big decision when we chose to double this core memory. We came to another decision point, what machine should we buy next? For reasons that are irrelevant, IBM people were tiresome in their salesmanship but we decided to buy an IBM 360. I told my computer manager, 'Tell IBM it's despite their salesmanship, not because of it'. Within two days, the UK managing director Ted Nixon (later to be knighted) was in my office to apologise. The signal had been transmitted, not smothered at local sales level, and rushed up the management tree despite any fear of blame or loss of face. I remain a staunch IBM admirer. How many large organisations could emulate that responsiveness?

In concordance with their policy IBM invited me to two free one-week courses on computing management for senior executives. Both were of the highest quality. These made clear that a computer application was determined by one guide – anything logical can be programmed, and by one major constraint, in practice, to exploit computing power fully is very difficult. The latter should be unsurprising. Tanks appeared in time for World War I but it was one thing to invent them and quite another to think through how to use them effectively.

IBM's guide through this blockage was stimulating. It may be as risky in terms of pay-off, said the instructor, to automate what is straightforward like payroll as to automate strategic decision-making like multi-factory production scheduling. The payroll would almost certainly work and save a few clerks; the scheduling may or may not work well but success would yield huge savings. In my time we used only limited imagination. I suspect we were not and are not alone. A few companies are exploiting this powerful instrument fully and with much profit while most find Information Technology too baffling. The eruption of IT into managers' lives is hard to handle – for all involved.

Having been made to write programmes (by IBM), I realise it is appallingly easy to make mistakes. When IBM ran my first programme the machine printed 'Mr Lyle has solved the wrong problem'. You must make, said IBM, your programmers 'document' their work. This they won't do voluntarily – it's boring to annotate their instructions so that a fresh programmer can follow what they've done. But how else can you de-bug a programme? Second, tell them what you want. If you don't, they will run the business, not you. Too true. My bank has automated its monthly statements. When I write against each cheque number the payee's name, I have to use a pen with a very fine nib: the programmer has defined too small a line spacing. I used to use Eurocheques abroad. The sum payable and the payee are allocated only the top third of the available space so overflows between sections can and do occur. Needless to say my complaints generate either hot air or silence. T & L created its own *faux pas.* A trainee manager recruited in the late autumn received in December this print-out, 'The Directors are pleased to inform you that your Christmas bonus is £0.00'. Of course the computer makers have something to answer for. My PC's instruction manual is quite clear – it's not an Amstrad! – but still has some notable omissions. Part is – to this baby – pure gobbledygook. I bought a new Word Processing programme for it and its manual was small help. I sent a long list of questions to the supplier; he said that I could pay £200 for an instruction course. It is interesting that what appear to be competent modem companies in a competitive business can manage such elementary errors. Philip and Oliver Lyle with Sir Noel Macklin built and sold the well known Invicta cars in the late twenties; Oliver wrote the instruction manual with his own hand.

Computer jokes are legion. It was said that IBM had a department whose sole job was to compose them. One of my instructors, Adrian Petch, told me he used to manage a computer department before joining IBM. He was warned the chairman was coming to inspect the strange beast they had bought. Petch took precautions. The great man arrived and was shown round. Through glazed eyes he stared mystified at the processor and the revolving tape drives. Petch pressed a button. The machine awoke. The printer rattled, 'Petch is a genius.' He nudged the chairman amiably in the ribs, 'It knows you see, Sir, it knows . . .'

13 Operations Research: A Tale of the Unexpected

In the late sixties we set up an OR Department. This discipline uses mathematics and logical thought to identify what is critical in an operation and thus be able to specify optimum conditions. In World War II its reputation was made by scientists like Blackett and Zuckerman. The former studied aircraft attacks on U-boats and was able to increase their lethality remarkably. Zuckerman deduced very practical techniques of aerial bombardment for interdiction purposes. Others could work out the optimum size for a convoy of merchantmen to minimise vulnerability to U-boats. After the war industry adopted OR but warily. One description of its methods was this, 'It's paying someone half your age to insult you.' Our department was managed by 'Long John' Tate, a mathematician of ability and charm. His high intelligence and integrity – which were only rivalled by his cookery skill – soon made the unit all and more than we expected. There were several reasons for a result which might well have been poor.

With his ability and name John operated without interference and without bureaucracy. He favoured smallness – the department was only three or four strong. He recruited only very bright people and they had to be practical. His selection technique, he told me, revolved around two questions only – the slightest whiff of airy-fairy politics and you were out. There was also a poser to be answered rapidly. You and your companion are dying of thirst in the desert; you find an irregularly shaped bottle and a chinagraph pencil, how do you divide the water exactly equally between you?*

---

*The answer is: One person takes a sip and marks the water level on the glass; the other person inverts the bottle, takes a sip and marks the level; each repeat the process alternately until the two levels coincide.

One recruit had been studying sub-atomic particles in their habitat at the bottom of India's deepest coalmine; these entertaining objects appeared, if memory serves, at the rate of two a month. The gentleman in question became T & L's Group Treasurer. The department's assignments were mostly conventional – vehicle routing, optimising stocks, raw sampling, etc. The scientists used a high level language (FORTRAN) for their computer programming, which saved work and being a small cohesive group could get away with minimal documentation. For the same reason the left hand knew what the right hand was doing. Such short cuts made for cost-effective work.

After a time we spotted OR people all over the place. Often a project was implemented and the customer said to John, 'I am impressed with your Mr X who has been helping us with the commissioning, can I keep him to run the system hereafter?' We had accidently acquired a selective recruitment and induction agency, which was at least as valuable as its nominal product. It is needless to remark that the department has long been disbanded.

14 Necessary Nitpickers

Over time the proportion of professional staff compared with total numbers has remorselessly increased. At a price this process has improved design, control and the ability to tackle esoteric problems or opportunities. I have comments on two types of specialist, both essential but both needing guidance or control. Both need precise minds, working to rules, and both can make indifferent managers. The result with engineers and accountants can be inveterate nit-picking by a stolid technician. But these have a role to play: someone must watch the rulebook, safety, cash flow, machine maintenance, housekeeping … The shift engineer in a cane sugar factory is an example. The first priority is keeping the mill going, otherwise costs go through the roof with spoiled cane, idle people and interest charges; fancy design is for someone else.

An accountant has been called the person who goes out onto the battlefield after the battle is over, counts the dead and bayonets the wounded. Robert Bruce writes (in *The Times*, 3 March 1994):

> Some [accountants] are enablers. Most are controllers . . . some accountants see their role as enabling an organisation to thrive, flourish and grow. The others see their purpose as simply putting the clammy hand of control over as much of the organisation as they possibly can.

Certainly bean counters promoted to positions of power have, I believe, damaged British industry. A short-term outlook, a concentration on the readily quantifiable at the expense of the intangible, a lack of empathy with people – these attitudes can cut the heart out of a company, especially when compounded by a recession.

T & L has mostly been very fortunate in its Finance Directors who have combined professional expertise with broad judgement but it has seldom allowed a senior accountant – termed a 'puff-adder' in the company patois – to run the business. But, like engineers, they have a place and can be used to much advantage. General von Hammerstein-Equord, one-time Chief of the German General Staff, summarises the matter (I quote from memory from a paper by Sir Frederick Hooper, then MD of what was then Schweppes Ltd):

> I divide my officers into four classes: the clever, the stupid, the industrious and the lazy. Every officer possesses at least two of these qualities. Those who are clever and industrious are fitted for high staff appointments. Use can be made of those who are stupid and lazy. The man who is clever and lazy is fitted for the highest command . . . But whoever is stupid and industrious is a danger and must be removed immediately.

I can't better that.

The German's profession exemplifies my point acutely. Our armed forces have been throughout the century at the mercy of politicians who, undeterred by a short-sighted public, demand budget savings. In both world wars they had to fight at the outset with inadequate resources and suffered death and wounds as a consequence. Quite unashamed by this, successive ministers of defence continue to cheese-pare and to shrug off the resulting over-stretch – with its stress on soldiers' marriages – and poor weaponry. Training in all services is curtailed. Accountants in Whitehall insist on smothering officers with paper-work in place of military preparedness and competence. Morale is dismal. What a way to run an organisation. Now lives are being lost.

When involved in running a company I felt keenly that a factory should not contain more than 500 people – some of ours had 2000 – if it were to be manageable for high morale, good productivity and simplicity. To an accountant the easily predictable extra fixed costs arising from extra sites was anathema; but that could be more than offset by such intangibles as higher productivity all the time, easier pay negotiations every year or avoiding a strike every five years or so, whose costs could readily offset the higher overhead. I still believe our Keynsham packing station (see section 9) exemplifies the point.

Plaistow had an exceptional Chief Engineer in John Carmichael, another relative. He had a strong personality and could handle and lead his staff; he knew his engineering; he had a marked flair for imaginative design. It was a pleasure to watch him sketch an engineering idea, done with the bold decisive strokes of the true artist. Tate's management could be eccentric and sometimes lacked chief executives of flair. It rightly sought to design a better cube making plant (the foundation of the Tates' prosperity) to make the hard, sparkling, quick-dissolving cube it had long marketed in preference to the modern 'pressed cube' now widely made by other companies and lacking these fine qualities. Tate's child, a right monster, would have made Heath Robinson feel totally outclassed.

I disgraced myself on seeing it for the first time by bursting out laughing. (Short) John Tate had shown it to the Belgian sugar refiners, who had a long tradition of cube making. I asked him what they thought of it. 'They just crossed themselves and went back to Belgium.'

15 Ideas for Management Organising

Textbook methods may not always be appropriate or the best. R K Mueller offers this for simplicity, 'African village organisation needed only one man: the rainmaker. When no rain came, the rainmaker was buried alive and a new one installed.'

The pairing of Refinery Directors has been mentioned. It yielded authority and decisiveness. It was also flexible. One person was usually the spokesman. One was often a young sprig learning the job. A twosome operated in other T & L areas, for example in Africa, where there were assets in South Africa, Zimbabwe and Zambia. Pairing reduced the travelling burden and provided continuity. A pair were often relatives or good friends. In those days the Board was a group of friends rather than just business colleagues, nor did control suffer thereby – leg-pulling and other exercising of friends' rights could be and was used, perhaps to greater effect than with a more formal group. The system accommodated eccentricity as well as talent. Oliver Lyle was a character as well as a fine sugar refiner. Latterly I was a junior director with him and knew him well. He remarked abruptly one day in his gravelly voice (he'd lost a vocal chord from cancer), 'Did you know that the seahorse lays 30,000 eggs and then turns black?' A pause. 'So should I if I'd laid 30,000 eggs!'

His wide interests embraced other biological curiosities. We were discussing human metabolism. There was a medical case, he said, which described a girl who only went to the loo once a year '. . . and then only produced a handful of dry husks'. I was reminded of this when at a party in Wallasey. The man I was talking to – an ex-brigadier and Jap POW – broke off to say: 'Do you see that small man over there, Fred X? Do you know, he only goes to the loo every two months.' I was intrigued. He went on, 'I was recently at a week-end party where Fred was also a guest. His time was approaching. A terrible tension hung over the whole place. Then on Sunday morning he disappeared for two hours, and came back looking absolutely radiant!' Two decades later I was at a wedding reception talking to my own family. I looked across the room. I said to my family, 'Do you see that small man over there? Well, he . . .'

Oliver had his blind spots. He and Ian Lyle were the Plaistow twosome after the war, to make a formidable pair. Being equal in seniority and ability, Ian became restless and wanted to take over or move. He raised the subject. Oliver said, 'But I've already handed over to you.'

The refinery organisation was simple. Under the two Refinery Directors was a Refinery Manager who had reporting to him a Process Manager, a Packing Manager, the Chief Chemist, the Chief Engineer, the Personnel Manager and an Administration Manager. The top arrangement, being one over one, unconsciously aped the military system. Just as the Army Commander has his Chief of Staff to put a smoothly running organisation at his disposal, so the Refinery Manager made the refinery routinely work, accommodating himself with agility to directors' whims and interference. As in the Army the director(s) had the time to talk to everyone, think up improvements, check on housekeeping and design strategy. Long before Peters and Waterman (in *In Search of Excellence* 1982) praised 'managing by walking about', T & L did it routinely.

The Process Manager managed production, the Chief Chemist quality, so the production man – tempted to favour output over quality – was not judge and jury; only his seniors could over-ride the chemist's quality decisions. But the Chief Engineer controlled maintenance when the Process Manager could better judge trade-offs between production revenue and repair costs. The Maintenance Engineer should have been accountable to the Process Manager for what he did and to the Chief Engineer (by a dotted line) for how he did it. Such organisational principles deserve attention.

The art is in balancing clarity with easy working. Too much administration stifles initiative. As Jack Welch says in *The Times*, 'Bureaucracy strangles. Informality liberates. Creating an informal atmosphere is a competitive advantage . . . It's about making sure everybody counts – and everybody knows the count.'

Perhaps that explains the point made by Peters and Waterman in *The Pursuit of Excellence*, '. . . the star performers are seldom led by accountants or lawyers.'

While talking of informality, here is another sort. The scene is a Royal Navy training establishment, HMS *Excellent*, built on a reclaimed island. Captain J G Wells writes in *The Naval Review*:

> As an acting Sub the writer can remember sitting on a wardroom earth closet early one morning to be startled by a voice from outside the back wall, 'Excuse me, sir – won't be a moment' as the bucket under the seat was deftly removed by a metal pole and hook, emptied into the horse-drawn sanitary cart and returned smartly with a cheery 'There we are, sir. All's well now!''

The cart in question was known as the Foo-Foo wagon.

16 Very Practical Statistical Techniques

Philip Lyle was a considerable mathematician and a Fellow of the Royal Statistical Society. As a direct result of his hobby T & L found numerous and beneficial applications for statistical techniques which otherwise might have escaped its attention. My father's interest had been long-lived. After the Great War he thought he'd invented a method of winning at a casino. The Board gave him six weeks' leave and he stayed in Monte Carlo, employing refugee aristocrats from

Bolshevik Russia to play the tables for him. His scheme was a complete failure but the weather was very agreeable.

His innovations at Plaistow fared better. He used regression analysis to derive correlations between variables, so deducing the division between fixed and marginal costs for pricing decisions and between fixed and variable fuel consumption for accurate product costing.

Plaistow was constantly experimenting with new plant or with process modifications to cut costs. The design of experiments by a statistician can make such investigation much more profitable. Suppose for example you want to investigate the effect on a product property of three variables, time, temperature and pressure. You should have three equally spaced time intervals, three equally spaced temperatures and three equally spaced pressures. There will be $3 \times 3 \times 3$ experiments yielding 27 results to consider but you are actually measuring the effect of time at 9 levels of temperature and at 9 pressures so are getting $9 \times 9 = 81$ results. As Oliver wrote in *Technology for Sugar Refinery Workers*, '... by adopting [what statisticians term] a "Factorial Design" we greatly reduce the actual number of experiments; we reduce the possibility of errors; we ascertain any interaction between the variables; and from the least possible number of experiments we can make the best estimate of the effect of each variable.'

Perhaps of wider interest is probability theory. If we toss a coin once, the probability of getting a head is a half or 50%, toss it twice and the chance of getting two heads is a quarter or 25% and so on. After seven throws the probability is down to less than 1 in a 100. But however rare, the chance may come up. As the statistician R A Fisher pointed out, you shouldn't be surprised at some remote event happening, only at it happening to you. For example, Oliver saw in the Small Arms Museum at Hythe the British rifle which was fired at the instant that a German bullet entered its muzzle. The barrel burst and the bullets rested point overlapping point! Very unlikely but it did actually happen. The practical aspect of probability theory is that one may have to repeat a test many times to get a 'statistically significant' result.

17 Management Consultants: Importing a Bomb Factory

At refinery and at company level we have used consultants, Anne Shaw, PE, PA, McKinsey and others – all well known. The biggest impact by far was made by Emerson Consultants, an American company, then headed in Britain by William Allen who had achieved public fame by his harsh criticism of British productivity. 'Half time Britain', he called us with pardonable exaggeration. Clearly he had character and imagination. I gave him a quick tour of Plaistow. He said, 'I don't know how you manage to employ so many people.' After top management had reached agreement, Emerson's assignment was defined as a self-contained local distribution study for the London refineries only. For this job Allen sent us two men, both very bright. They went to work.

One, Dr Robert Gregory (author of a classic book on Data Processing) slipped into Plaistow's office at dawn when the '6 to 2 shift' was commencing its labours and made concise notes of all the activity he could observe in the yard below him where trucks were normally being loaded with sugar. He read out to us what he had seen from his window:

6 am Nothing happening.

6.10 Nothing happening.

6.20 A man crosses the yard.

6.30 Someone transports a can of tea . . .

He proceeded mercilessly in similar fashion for some considerable time. We writhed but we got the message. Totally ignoring the delimiting of their brief the pair ranged in all directions, probing refinery director competence, export marketing performance, company attitudes and production scheduling. They also looked at London refinery distribution, the job they had been asked to do!

All this caused the biggest row on the Board I ever saw. But confronted with uncomfortable facts we listened to them and got off our backsides. The pair came to interview me as the 'production director' on the scope for automating process operations, for enhanced productivity and plant utilisation. With shame I can remember telling them there was no scope. Within weeks they had me in the USA looking at a computer controlled paper mill in Pennsylvania and at an automated process for making synthetic rubber in Louisiana. The notice board outside the latter factory bore plots of local hurricane tracks to warn employees to care for their homes. I stayed in a local motel and read a book during supper. The delightful waitress said to me, 'I see ya readin' a book. Ah'm readin' a book too.'

The moral of the story is simple. The consultant is the only person who can tell the boss he's an ass.

18 The Case for Consultants

In some ways consultants are debilitating. They may feed back to you – for a fee – what they have learned from your own staff. I have yet to meet one who used consultants to improve *his* consultancy; consultants are for others to employ. Some pride themselves on implementing their recommendations and not leaving you to continue alone. I suggest there is another side to this. If you have to see through what they and you have agreed in principle then in the process you will acquire a capacity for yourself. Next time you can go it wholly alone. The consultancy will have set up the patient to heal himself from now on. That could be worth quite a substantial fee.

Apart from this and from an independent outsider's ability – which he may or may not exercise in practice – to shake up top management, a competent consultant can offer some specific aids:

- A temporary staff resource, hand-picked for a particular talent.

- A fresh viewpoint, stimulated by previous contact with other organisations having analogous problems and opportunities.

- Specialised knowledge.

- An aid to innovation: 'a prophet is not without honour . . . etc.'

- A sounding board for staff worries and morale.

- Private aid and comfort to a lonely boss.

These offerings are mostly obvious. To expand on the last point, there are topics a senior manager or director may wish to discuss with someone knowledgeable but independent, without exposing himself to company politics. The subject may be someone's promotion, an organisational change, a personal problem, company morale, or whatever. The consultant in this situation is someone paid to listen to you; if he is sympathetic and experienced and tactful he could be extremely valuable. A day's private session, perhaps twice a year, would be cheap at the price.

The only other point I have is that there are horses for courses with consultants. Some are good at this while being (surprisingly) bad at that. It is worth shopping around. But the potentially most valuable contribution by far is to place a bomb under the complacency of top management. The problem then is, how to recruit this corporate terrorist when the boss won't? Temporary help to handle a short term overload is an excuse. Or managers may propose – as ours did – a seemingly confined and harmless consultancy project and hope a latterday Emerson will sap and mine!

Sometimes, it seems, consultants sell themselves. I understand Marks & Spencer has employed many such recently, and not in series either. Even, it is said, a consultant to advise on the use of consultants. There is the makings of an infinite regress here: why not a consultant to advise on a consultant to advise on . . . ad infinitum?

19 Training as an Investment

It was not until I left T & L and worked with a training company that I realised how deficient training in British industry was and, despite employee demand and other pressures, still is. It was looked on as an inessential cost and a person sent on a course, which taught him or her something to apply back at work, usually had re-entry problems. To spend money you grudge and then reject the product takes some doing. Trish Nicholson in *The Times* wrote, 'A recent survey by the Alfred Marks Group revealed that 67% of managers interviewed had not applied what they had learned on courses. Another 23% had made no attempt to do so, and the remaining 44% had been unable to because of "the entrenched attitudes of bosses, company power structure and lack of resources".'

Training needs to be managed, like other activities. A course is to be an investment of time and money to obtain a defined improvement in efficiency or skill or knowledge, with feedback to check on the return. Has the course paid off? If not, who is at fault? T & L did not do this; even though it was doing more and more training it was really then playing at it.

The services do not play at it. Most of the time they have nothing else to do. Furthermore, they can only put into practice what they have learned or thought about every twenty years or so when they have a real war and can test theory and equipment. To mitigate the huge difficulties of this position, which industry does not suffer from at all, constant preparation, thinking, simulation, and mock trials is all that can be done. This makes the services very good trainers. My father explained their situation. Suppose, he said, you are an 'armed service company' but making sugar. Most years you make no sugar. For two weeks each year you go on 'manoeuvres' and make dummy sugar. Umpires tell you if this tastes like real sugar. Then every twenty years or so, war is declared, it's a national emergency, you are to make huge amounts of real sugar instantly and it must be better than the enemy's. Your slim factory staff, the 'regulars', are supplemented by large numbers of conscripted civilian refiners who must be trained in short order to boil sugar, filter it, pack it . . . all with professional skill. What a scenario! Thank Heaven we in industry don't have it. If we did, we might take training more seriously.

I would like to advocate one particular simulation for industry to ease a tension between participants. Trade union power is not what it was but worker suspicions remain, not without reason. There are good management games in which students act as top managers of competing companies. The combative situation makes for high motivation. In a student group of fifteen or twenty people, you can have a mixture of knowledge and seniority from the top to the shop floor. Now give each company a continuing objective: A is to maximise shareholders' profit in the long term; B is to maximise customer satisfaction; C is to maximise the long term wages and salaries of employees. All go to work and compete over say a 'ten year period'. At close of play there is a thorough post-mortem. I suggest all groups will find that they adopted *identical* specific objectives designed to fulfil the differing overall missions. Mutual support will be found to have benefited all stakeholders. The common ground so identified should be striking. It becomes explicit that maximising the shareholders' return, customer satisfaction and staff incomes are all necessary conditions for success. Putting it another way, these three factors are what we mean by a good company.

20 Managerial Fashions

I have seen panaceas for troubled managers come and go. Management-by-Objectives, Strategic Planning, Organisation Development, Performance Pay, Work Study . . . and so on. They were usually plugged by well-known gurus and, to busy managers not too ready to question them, these schemes appeared potentially helpful and pleasingly 'with-it'. Most have evaporated but the concept lives on. To inoculate ourselves against such bugs here is a modern example to bear in mind. The extract was taken from *The Director* and the writer is Michael Blakstad, chief executive of a company producing TV and communications programmes for other companies,

> . . . the television industry . . . has down-sized to the point where over half its workforce are either freelance or in tiny 'service' companies. Mission accomplished? . . . the signs are ominous . . . [the author's company, Workhouse] stands to gain from 'outsourcing' . . . When corporate clients closed their in-house video units, Workhouse inherited the workload. Encouragingly, we are now being asked [by companies who] have shed the managers who had previously supervised our work . . . to 'behave as though we were members of the firm and not as outside suppliers'.. .
>
> It is dangerous in this day and age to cry 'halt' in the face of a ravening management fashion. Nonetheless, this backwoodsman wants to turn the tide. Any business contemplating drastic reductions of staff and outsourcing of services should first examine the effect these policies are having on television. For a start, who offers career guidance for those who want to join the industry? Where do the Lumpenproletariat receive their training? . . . Colleges would like to fill gaps in training and career guidance, but slimmed-down companies aren't able to offer the kind of advice and facilities which the colleges need . . . Then, who takes risks in the freelance culture? . . . Freelances are averse to risk-taking since they know their next job depends on the success of their last one. Still less are they likely to be critical of their

employees – yet upwards appraisal is one of the most important organisms in a healthy company.

The ideal lies somewhere between the over-populated company of the eighties and the current cult of the mean machine. If the down-sized, outsourced skeleton operation is regarded as a temporary necessity and not as a goal in itself, and if companies learn to treat their suppliers as members of an extended family and not as monkeys on a leash, then the excesses of the overstaffed past can be avoided without resorting to scorched earth policies. . . . We must, however . . . offer a unique and competitive service. We'll only do that profitably if our own people have those skills and they are retained within the company . . . Our people really are our most valuable asset, and they're only truly ours when they are dedicated to us and we to them. I hope I won't then be treated to lectures about the need to remain right-sized, out-sourced and callous.'

The message is simple – think through the consequences of that fresh, dynamic and macho policy of yours. Don't over-simplify. What may happen in the long-term? A 'scorched earth' strategy may rejuvenate the bottom line today but industry must have a vested interest in social stability and cohesion continuing into tomorrow.

Chapter III

Directing a Family (or Other) Business

'I learned just by going around. I know all about Kleenex
factories, and all sorts of things.'

– The Princess Royal

21 Family Directors Only?

Exclusivity of appointment must be a function of circumstances. My
present personal partnership is composed of family only. My little
sweetener company has three family and one non-family directors.
T & L derived high talent from promoting non-family members.
Anyway, in a large company with many such, they deserve and
demand an incentive, a reward and significant participation.

Even the still small Abram Lyle company with a plethora of family
talent appointed a very able outsider, Julius Runge and father of Sir
Peter, in 1921 to manage raw sugar purchasing – for the company a
critical area. It had no regrets. In fact the Runge family with its
ability became close associates. Peter and his son Charles both
enjoyed privileged entry almost as Lyles – a further example of
flexibility.

45

There may well be cases where the family needs help or force to sort out problems. (Perhaps because it hasn't followed Sam Goldwyn's advice? 'I don't want any yes-men around me. I want everybody to tell me the truth even if it costs them their jobs.') T & L did so in the seventies. The families simply had not run the company well enough to maintain their pervasive influence in a large growing publicly owned organisation – not a unique situation. Saatchi & Saatchi appear to have survived a crisis with its non-executive directors heavily involved. The then extended Clarke family suffered dissent about the shoe business, which could have indicated the need for an outside agent to assist resolution. (This could have been an opportunity for that keen believer heard in prayer by Anon: 'Use me as you will, O Lord, but preferably in an advisory capacity.') One suspects that in all such cases what was hitherto a family business can't regain that status, once lost. The process of such evolution is irreversible.

T & L's Board met at 'Head Office', an old fashioned and quite handsome building in Mincing Lane. It was no doubt traditional in staffing and custom. There was a pleasing story, which I was never able to verify, that in the 1st Floor Gents used by senior people, staff had to stand and perform downstream of directors.

The message from all this is that if you want to preserve the status of a family business, a clear strategy defining size, growth, profitability, recruitment, capital sourcing and so on is the only safe assurance for the long term.

22 One Boss or Two?

Where there is a separate managing director (MD) or chief executive (CE) the chairman's role is pervasive, varied but clear:

To 'manage' the Board: appointments, removal of members, organisation of meetings and their agenda, seniors' remuneration, etc.

To guide, advise and observe the CE on behalf of the Board.

To help or complement the CE's work in any respect that seems desirable.

To represent the company to outsiders: shareholders, the media, institutional investors, politicians.

To perform ceremonial.

To keep in touch with and be known to all levels of staff.

The CE's job is to recommend policies, strategies and plans to the Board and to implement what it decides through his management team. His is thus a quite different role from the chairman's, though the two are complementary; they therefore call for different sets of abilities. For one person to accommodate both sets would be unusual.

For much of my time T & L had no CE. We were all executive directors. This was enjoyable but not too efficient. Only the chairman was (informally) *primus inter pares*. He was full-time but no one person was responsible for ensuring that everything was being attended to by someone. This was a serious weakness. For years Ian Lyle, chairman for a stimulating decade, resisted all proposals for a change. His argument was simple – creating a CE would concentrate too much power in one person's hands. The case had substance but was, I believe, exaggerated and Ian ignored his own power which was considerable. After all, by resisting a CE he was demonstrating the very concentration of power which concerned him.

His argument applies *a fortiori* against combining chairman and CE roles, anyway in large companies. The person becomes judge and jury. He may not be equally proficient at both roles. There is no one formally able to guide or intervene – though a forceful non-executive director (NED) *may* fill the gap though this is unlikely. There are cases of a group of NEDs over-throwing a chairman-cum-CE but this may very well not provide the on-going surveillance of or assistance to the CE *qua* CE. He can't guide himself. In any case the damage may by then be done.

If a company is too rigid or its Board too large and extended, informal subversion will occur. In Ian's time a small group of senior directors met in the evening and dissected the business; others heard about it afterwards. It is an example of Churchill's shrewd observation: 'It is in the nature of executive power to draw itself into the smallest possible compass.' This as in our case may be a necessary palliative, even if it is not the proper cure. The Board was a large group of active equals and resembled Britain's government in the Great War, described by Churchill thus:

> Whereas practically all the important matters connected with the war had been dealt with in the late Government by four or five Ministers, at least a dozen powerful, capable, distinguished personalities who were in a position to assert themselves had now to be consulted. The progress of business therefore became cumbrous and laborious in the last degree . . . (quoted from *The World Crisis*)

A small inner Cabinet or executive committee, chaired by the CEO, is a solution but does nothing for another problem – solving today's difficulties with yesterday's methods. As those past practices worked very well in their time, this reinforces the hiatus. T & L experienced this. After the war Ian Lyle and Peter Runge wrote a private paper addressed to the Board, which recommended (very sensible and overdue) changes in Board practice, training and policy. It was labelled The Great Sedition; Leonard Lyle, later a peer and our then president, labelled it, 'a bunch of platitudes.' Much of it was discreetly if slowly implemented. The next generation repeated the technique – only to be greeted in its day with Ian's and Peter's staunch resistance. I'm sure I copied this syndrome in my time! Anyway, innovation resulted. Subversion can be a useful and necessary supplement to other more respectable improvement processes.

23 Changing Chairmen

I became a director of T & L and attended my first board meeting in 1954. That same evening I found myself with most of my new colleagues at a further (informal) meeting in my father's London flat. The only absentees were the chairman, Vernon Tate, and Ian Lyle. My father, as senior director, informally chaired the proceedings. There was, he said, a general feeling on the Board that Vernon, who had been chairman for a long time, could sensibly be replaced by Ian (clearly there had been informal soundings). My father proposed that for a smooth transition Vernon be asked to become President while Ian took the chairmanship. Would this be acceptable to Vernon? Yes, said Tony Tate, he thought it would (the presidency had little power but much dignity and was not necessarily a sinecure; it kept Vernon's ideas and experience, which were considerable, available to the company).

All being agreed, the meeting broke up. Within days the decisions were implemented without fuss or argument or public clamour – an example for Lord Howe *et al* relative to Lady Thatcher.

The process was repeated much later when John Lyle, then chairman, was under a strain which he could not recognise. Ian, then an elder statesman, initiated informal discussions which lead to the replacement of John with Lord Jellicoe. The method is therefore workable even when the parties are rather unwilling. It does, I admit, presuppose the Board's containing some independent-minded members but directors should always be that. A political party may find such a system clashing with a modern open consultative election, but neither of the major parties have found their respective methods to work with consistent or even significant success.

George Jellicoe had been an NED for some years before assuming the chair. His most memorable communication occurred when we were embroiled in an endless argument with Iran for whom we were conducting a large raw sugar trading operation. The Iranians viewed us with high suspicion: it seemed inconceivable that our arguments and statements were honourable and not self-seeking. George nicely articulated our frustrations when he informed a board meeting that there was this saying extant in the Middle East, 'When you kick an Iranian up the arse you lose your boot.'

24 Non-Executive Directors: For and Against

The case for NEDs is straightforward – independence, outside contacts and knowledge, non-departmental outlook, special experience. Sir Owen Green amongst others has argued that their serious weakness is ignorance. In my admittedly limited experience I believe he is right. T & L has had NEDs for four decades. Some arrived through acquisitions, others from old boy networks. Most were able. All contributed something, if only useful contacts or knowledge but this was of limited benefit and none could really hold an initiative over a competent insider. They did not tour the company on appointment so didn't know a sugar refinery from a sewage works. My grapevine tells me there was one notable exception: Lady Prior insisted on making an extensive tour.

Attending for a monthly Board meeting – plus perhaps one day a month as a member of a remuneration or audit committee – simply could not brief them. They appeared collaborators with the chairman – which perhaps gave him useful support vis-à-vis inside directors but didn't make for cohesion. When recommending their colleagues' remuneration, as they do in many companies, they seem interested parties. Many are CE's themselves and anyway are beholden to the chairman for their NED job. Independent? The current level of seniors' pay, often justified by referring to 'market rates', is sufficient comment. Commenting on the insiders' reward being, apart from salary, payments by way of bonuses and share options, Sir Owen

Green, in *The Director* comments: 'But the combination of the two represents a double-dip into the barrel of available incentive monies. It must be divisive, inflationary and, for as long as it is available, greed-promoting. There is little proof of its effectiveness in relation to management performance.'

To compound the mischief our NEDs often acquired only nominal shareholdings in T & L when a serious part of their job was to look after investors' interests. For example, in 1991 of the six NEDs only two had holdings of over 2,000 ordinary shares.

Against all this, insider directors have their own weaknesses. They are even more beholden to the CE or chairman, having more at stake. They tend to think first of their departments, not of overall strategy. They get appointed through being good senior managers when, as my father preached, you promote a person, not because he is good in his present job, but because he should be good in his next. The role of a manager accountable directly for a particular unit in all respects does not encourage his making a good company director.

To solve this conundrum requires change. NEDs are needed to extend a board's resources and vision and a mix with insiders can make for balance and be fruitful, but the NEDs must have time to find out what is going on and to understand those aspects that are critical for the company's success at top management level. They need also some independence vis-à-vis the chairman/CE. Against such a background they can make their contribution. What precisely is this?

I suggest it is not his or her contacts. The insiders can have these in sufficiency, indeed should be encouraged to have them as part of their job and their personal development. There may be special cases for a NED's friends but this is unusual. So contacts should score low marks in the selection. What of special expertise? Unless there is a continuing and pervasive need for this to inform and underwrite much Board business, such input can be more neatly provided by consultants and for short terms.

Then what about care of stakeholders' interests? Reassurance of interested but discrete bodies – shareholders, customers, the public, government – by outsiders contributing integrity, disinterested comment, prestige, and unsolicited independent analysis – all this sounds a good thing. But here be dragons. A director has power and influence; he can give his views unasked, even interfere without permission. This makes him in one respect good for the company and beneficial to the external publics. But to do this effectively he must know what he is doing and act with tact.

This calls for knowledge, to know what to look at and for, and for the time to acquire this knowledge and to make his views known. Companies can be seriously heterogeneous without being a conglomerate, with more than one core business and with a geographical spread that poses its own special problems. To be informed on such as this is a considerable task. T & L as it now is exemplifies this. So the NED cannot be the (busy) executive of another company, much less its CE. He can be a professional NED if really independent – i.e. rich enough not to care overmuch about his fee. He can be a management consultant, used to deriving performance appraisals from quick over-views. To be really free from financial pressure he should not be paid by the company but by, say, a group of institutional investors; a competent person observing and serving their interests by encouraging improvements would be cheap at the price. Other professionals – redundant managers with free time, lawyers, ex-civil servants, retired servicemen – could equally find a similar role to play. However, and this is a major proviso, the NED and the insider must share a common continuing objective – the long term performance of the company and be at ease with each other. A Board split between a bunch of doers and a cluster of watchdogs would be too like the House of Commons to perform.

25 A Really Useful Director

One T & L director can appear to conform to this standard NED specification we have arrived at. Saxon Tate had twenty-five years training and executive experience in all parts of the Group, ending up as CE. With his astonishing learning capacity, his relations with staff at all levels, the time he had to tour the Group routinely, his outside experience in North Ireland government and City trading, and you have an admirably qualified individual. His private means fortifies him to lift two fingers to the company if he feels like it but his long standing relations – formal and informal – with the management makes this a theoretical point. What more can you want? In short, the ex-insider with these appurtenances is potentially the most effective NED.

He has another advantage. Sir Owen Green warns against 'an over-emphasis on monitoring'; if corporate governance increasingly distinguishes between NEDs and insiders, 'It will lead to a distinction of purpose and, sooner or later, of behaviour.' He goes on to argue that if there are to be three or more NEDs on a typical large company Board the outcome may not be what is intended, 'That there should be at least three 'watchdogs' . . . renders more and more remote the idea of a thrusting, innovative, creative group of people'.

Losing the profits baby with the surveillance bath water is not going to benefit anyone. I have already mentioned T & L's Board being – in earlier times – a group of friends. This made for a highly congenial cohesion and kept company politics within comfortable bounds. The results were not as productive as those splendid ones from Sir Owen's own BTR Board as it was then, but that does not negate his point or mine. The more I think about it the more cogent does the Green thesis appear to be. He would look to the auditors, already meant to be wholly independent of management, to check on financial rectitude in the shareholders' interests, so reducing the NEDs 'watchdog' role and in turn the divisive behaviour he fears.

This would (broadly) serve to mitigate the hurt from fiddling or incompetence but not much more. I suspect to do much better, to be warned of foreseeable company failures by shrewd NED-like observers, is not to be attained reliably. Then why risk the Green disease? After all, even insiders can be bamboozled. A senior McKinsey consultant told me that his very first assignment was a general survey of a substantial company. He concluded that it was rushing to ruin. He presented his findings to the Board. The directors had only one question: 'How long have we got?'

To reinforce the argument, surveillance is simply not of universal appeal. I knew of a company with a Board of the great and the good – very senior politicians and ex-servicemen and suchlike. The company was bankrupt and up for sale at a distressed price. Another company bought it and as its subsidiary it lives on – with the same Board in place.

26 'Acquired' Directors

As part of a merger or takeover deal Board appointments may be given or received. T & L thus acquired several directors. They came equipped with some knowledge of the business we had bought but sometimes with not much else. But that equipment alone was worth something. Takeovers were fashionable; they satisfied managers' lust for size; managements in their arrogance then and now think they can run someone else's business better than he can; takeovers appear to buy market share cheaply. I suggest all these arguments are largely specious and that most takeovers fail to benefit the acquiring company's shareholders. There are notable exceptions to this rule: Hanson and BTR to name but two, show how it can be done profitably – anyway for a bit! Most of T & L's sallies into diversification proved failures. The recent chairman, Neil Shaw, has sensibly culled the flock so as to concentrate on core business.

I have one other comment. When T & L acquired control of a

Canadian refiner – the Canada & Dominion Sugar Company (C & D) – it replaced (without a row) the somewhat eccentric CE with its own nominee. This was Jo Whitmee, a senior full-time executive T & L director. He was a born manager, more so than any person I have known. His high inborn talent and charm commanded universal respect. His being at the time our ablest Board executive derived in part from his insight and his lovableness: he was astonishingly empathetic. Installed without any rancour in C & D, he set himself up, not as the British appointee, but as the Canadian leader; 'C & D' was written across his chest. He won its trust and affection in short order while continuing to hold T& L's complete confidence. While the C & D Board continued to exist, with a mix of insiders, Canadian NEDs and T & L appointees other than Jo, this was not the main buttress of mutual confidence. It was Jo's ability, his T & L directorship with its power, his weekly personal letters to our chairman to supplement his formal communications, that maintained C & D's morale and T & L's relaxed delegation to its Board.

It exemplified an optimistic angle on a point already raised – the Green disease. The Board represented Canadian shareholders, then a large minority, as well as meeting local Canadian concerns about employment and foreign takeovers and French Canadian sensitivities. It had a large refinery in Montreal. The Board under its Canadian chairman in my direct experience, was cohesive, friendly, constructive, active and well informed. The management were notably innovative and enterprising. I think this exception to the Green 'rule' was due to a combination of factors. We all knew each other well and met socially as well as at work; we knew many of the C & D managers; we had Canadian connections; we knew or learned the business. Neil Shaw, the then CE, routinely arranged instructive visits after every Board meeting to a C & D office or plant. None of these supports were special to us, others could copy. The whole set-up seems an object lesson in how to manage a proud acquisition in a distant land.

But the acquisition had been gentle. It had been preceded by a consultancy in the fifties when we contributed advice on the design of C & D's new refinery on the Toronto waterfront. The friendly relations made for mutual acquaintance and confidence. Of the latter I can give one example. Ian Lyle visited the refinery during construction; its boilers were being erected but their insides were visible. Ian, looking at the tubing implanted in the combustion chamber walls, said to his guide, C & D's chief engineer, 'Doesn't it normally run vertically rather than horizontally?' Jack Swan was somewhat taken aback at a company chairman's knowledge.

27 The Usefulness of Subsidiary Boards

C & D was a subsidiary company, T & L then owning only 56% of the equity. To maintain its Canadian appearance and standards, its having a Board accommodated Canadian personalities, one as chairman. With its T & L appointees it provided a convenient vehicle for managing a distant province through its own satrap. Importantly, local sensibilities and concerns, the morale of the staff, the accommodation of local minority interests, are all recognised and assuaged.

A 100% subsidiary in the UK can also have a useful Board and several T & L ones did so. The management structure was simple. Each division had in T & L a 'Divisional Director' (DD) reporting to the main Board. Subsidiary company managers reported to the DD. The subsidiary Board was 'alongside' the DD on the organisation chart, having a responsible role to play, advising and monitoring, yet not clouding the accountability of the DD.

To save regulatory and accounting fees the subsidiary board need not be a legal entity. It contributes several managerial advantages:

- The Divisional Director, usually its chairman, can have advice from insiders and outsiders, just as at main Board level.

- The Board can as a group be exposed to disciplines: e.g. monthly cash flow analysis, sales reports, capital spending reports.

- In return for these influences, these checks and balances, T & L will be encouraged to award more authority than it would to an isolated (lonely) individual; it is thus an instrument of delegation.

- It gives directorial experience to middle managers as well as the prestigious label of 'Director'.

- It exposes insiders' Board performance to view – an aid to appraising their potential.

- It may confer unit identification and pride, being a profit centre, not a cost centre.

In total these add up to a worthwhile benefit. Of these, I would rate most highly the prestige and pride conferred on the unit and the prodding to increase delegation by the Board. Both are delicate plants, needing constant nurturing and nudging.

28 T & L's Board: Growth or Control?

Our collection of directors – for most of my time family plus some senior managers plus one or two NEDs – made for a curious mix of collective conservatism and individual enterprise. The two families had joined forces in 1921 under the pressure of severe competition. The union flourished and for five decades grew in size and profits yet, as already mentioned, Philip and Oliver Lyle had opposed the marriage: they foresaw the ending of Abram Lyle as a family business. It took time – just one generation before finality.

Although Tate sold twice as much sugar their profits only equalled Lyle's; in addition they had two refineries to our one. Nevertheless, the merger was, very gratifyingly, on a 50/50 basis. It took literally years to combine the two operations given a past of secrecy, rivalry and differing cultures. The Tates employed professional mangers; the Lyles did their own managing. Both had technical strengths and weaknesses though the Lyles knew more of what was going on; Tate was perhaps more market oriented. The Tates had charm and were nicer, '. . . those bloody Lyles!' We were tougher and did not accept too readily what managers proposed. Though close friendships developed no inter-marriage has ever happened.

Before the amalgamation there had been hardly a single instance of any contact between the families. Plaistow kept up the barricades. In 1928 T & L bought up the refining business of Fairrie & Sons of Liverpool. Geoffrey Fairrie, a very sound and practical sugar refiner, told me that before the buy-out he had asked his father to arrange for him to see round Plaistow. For weeks he heard nothing. He reminded his father, who replied: 'The Lyles say, "tell us when Geoffrey is coming and we'll be waiting for him with a shot-gun".'

T & L Board meetings were fortnightly. Members knew each other intimately. There was, as has been noted, some subversion and politicking but this was done in moderation. Friendliness prevailed, perhaps helped because central direction could afford to be a light touch when competition was gentle. Directorial debates could be vigorous but were never put to a vote. Except once. This concerned a triviality – should a report on the AGM go in the Yorkshire Post? A majority were in favour but the voting was against because one elderly director had misheard the resolution – which the Secretary then misinterpreted and bought space for the report!

Later the Board became less of a group of friends and no family business at all. No doubt it is now broader based and more open-minded, perhaps more thrusting and agile. I am hardly unbiased but both the old and the new had or have merit. The family-dominated Board was pretty open to argument and avoided much personal rivalry but could and did hanker after employing successful past practice which time had since made obsolete. Very free from politicking it could yet resist change. Between us we knew a lot about the business which was run – for good or ill – in a very personal way. This was its distinguishing characteristic. Of course non-family businesses can tap employee enthusiasm by good management. Here is an example of just that from Nuclear Electric, David Young writes in *The Times*:

> At one station, the bill for repairing a leak in the turbine pipework was cut by an estimated £3.5 million when one of the control-room staff suggested that he used his pot-holing skills to hang upside down for five hours inside the turbine to repair pipework. This would normally have involved a complete closure of the station . . .

Now corporate direction is (to my mind) much too impersonal and pays only lip-service to long-term activities like research but authority appears clear-cut and the organisation streamlined, with systematic handling of – for example – PR and shareholder relations. It certainly makes much more money yet contrives to have a high turnover in top management. New managements are always tempted to pour scorn and derision on the previous one but to announce – as the new T & L one did to demonstrate its crusading zeal – that it had replaced all the Rolls-Royces with Fords – was a slight exaggeration when there had been not a single Rolls to replace.

This ultimate outcome was probably the inevitable fruit of the amalgamation with Tate. Philip and Oliver were far-sighted. It is a matter of personal objective. If you want personally to create a fine empire with its appropriate style of managing, that is one thing and perfectly consistent. If in contrast you want your own business which can be handed on to your children and grandchildren, that is quite another. For that you may well have to forsake growth, certainly growth for its own sake, and instead pursue like the Greeks excellence rather than size – but then a fine family property is a highly rewarding legacy. In our case I believe the turning point after the amalgamation was the purchase of United Molasses. It was a large public company and successful too. We acquired it when its share price was hit by a temporary slump in molasses prices and freight rates. Its purchase heavily diluted the family holdings, brought in two NEDs onto our Board and involved us in a business we knew little about. We were fooled by thinking that because we produced a lot of molasses as a by-product we knew about its trading. Only the secondment of our senior and extraordinarily able buyer, Michael Attfield, restored the situation. I had been the sole opponent of the takeover in the Board's lengthy debate on the move. I feared the end of the family business but was out-voted on the argument that it would be good for our shareholders who were of course in a large majority. If we had not joined up with Tate we would not have got into the position where the majority were right and I was wrong. UM's current main claim to fame is that one of its senior people was recently stopped by the police for speeding on the M4 while using his carphone and eating a ham sandwich.

29 Seniors' Workload Problems

If drawing a bead on an invisible Rolls was shooting at an ephemeral target, the error is very understandable. The new management of T & L took over because the previous one – us, the families – could have run the company better and had no sufficient shareholding to resist a change, had we wished to. Sir Neil Shaw, now as well known in the UK as in his native Canada, by hands-on management converted a too diverse, ill-focused group into a world-wide sweetener company in an astonishingly short time. His drive, decisiveness and highly deft footwork must have been enormously demanding in time, energy, resilience and thought – which itself encroaches further on available time. Against this considerable achievement are to be set only minor irritations or mistakes.

Evading them takes time – which is in short supply. Rapidly to improve the P & L Account the new management ordered universal economy-class travel, not so much to save money as to signal a sea-change in attitude. I emerged from the rear of a 747 at Toronto for my next C & D Board meeting to collide with two senior directors coming from the nose. Time spent thinking beforehand could have disclosed that a simple general edict has faults; a selective one, which has to be thought through, would have recognised that the strength and comfort of those few with many major tasks on their shoulders is well worth sustaining and is aided by minimising the stress and discomfort of frequent long range flights. In addition, sitting up front can provide useful business contacts and an opportunity to catch up on work. Perhaps more important to top managers is the comfort, service and quiet. If no urgent work beckons, you can sit and think ... or prepare for a forthcoming meeting. What better way to refute the nit-picking of the bean counters?

But time to think, except when air travel imposes it, is what seniors don't have, especially those as in our case were engineering major changes. I am convinced industry grossly overloads its top people. They are made to feel accountable to their Boards or the media or the City or institutions – or all! For such wide and deep responsibilities they work flat out – perhaps too often on the urgent rather than on the important. With a superfluity of legislation and increasing pressures from environmental and other social interests, just keeping their empire's nose clean must be a continuing and worrying load superimposed on their conventional managerial objectives. It can be no surprise that they take packed brief cases home, neglect their families, their outside contacts and their own interests, as well as their health and their personal financial affairs. After retiring I spent a whole week on my Inheritance Tax planning; I simply could not have found the time when in regular work. The result for the employee is a company's man, far too dependent on his salary and pension – in short, a yes-man, which is the last thing the company needs!

With more free time created for him he could mitigate these

difficulties and do better quality work into the bargain. These huge benefits a proved system could well provide.

30 'Mission Impossible?'

The overload for top management is serious now and getting worse. The implications for its selection, supervision, remuneration and supply must raise vital questions for all 'stakeholders'. Professor Bennis of the University of Southern California in an article by Desmond Dearlove in *The Times*, says,

> a more clogged cartography of stakeholders, unbelievable changes, disruptive technologies, globalisation, inflection points no one would even think about ten years ago and most of all speed. It not only takes a strong stomach and a tough nervous system but a mind that can take nine points of view and connect the dots ... I am certain it is the selection process that is at fault ... boards who go into rhapsodic and romantic overtures about leadership never really define what they mean by that word nor do they pay enough attention to the human factor.

He thinks a CEO now needs twice the time of a few years ago to master his job. He is expected 'to know exactly what [he] should do in any situation', says Professor Steele from Cranfield School of Management, when he doesn't. Yet he cannot admit to such ignorance for fear of looking weak or incompetent.

Despite these pressures there is no lack of volunteers for the job. As the supply of exceptional talent is limited and inelastic (in the sense that mere pay will not readily increase the supply) the hunt for it intensifies, its remuneration rises (to bribe people to take a job they cannot comfortably do) and its breeding is now to be studied. Meantime, it seems that only making the real situation clear and having it accepted by stakeholders, with a supportive Board and chairman and a subtle system of delegation plus responsible staff support, can make the business work in tolerable fashion. If naught positive can be done and the trend continues, the role may become impossible. Is it now? 'Not yet,' says Professor Steele, 'but we are on the verge.'

31 A Solution: the Chief of Staff System

The working of the Army's method for easing a commander's workload is very well illustrated by General Montgomery's appointment to take over command of the 8th Army in August 1942. The Germans had by then driven it back almost in rout to El Alamein, a mere thirty miles from Cairo, to leave it brave but bewildered, experienced yet inexpert, out-numbering its enemy but out-fought by him, and without inspiration and stability. As I explain in a book *What The Civilian Manager Isn't Taught*, Monty's brief was simple:

> . . . to learn all about the area, [he had never been to Egypt] to defeat any enemy attacks, to study foe and friends – leaders, morale, resources, organisation, tactics, skills – to evaluate these factors, to improve any on his side that were deficient and to design and execute an offensive and pursuit to eject the Axis totally and for good from the Western Desert. If all that took more than a few months he would be deemed a failure.

It actually took him 23 weeks and 3 days.

Every Army Commander had a chief of staff, whose job it was to put a smoothly running organisation at the Army Commander's disposal for the execution of his policy and plans. The Chief of Staff handled routine administration, planning, and the detail of execution. For Monty his staff's work included battle plans for each corps, deception schemes, training, forming a port reconditioning team, supply dump building, the assessment of Libyan terrain – amongst other matters. This freed the Commander to do the work *only he could do*: appraising the army's leaders and the enemy potential, designing strategy, improving morale and his command's PR, handling ceremonial as well as personal presentations. In short, for him it was first things first and all the time.

It didn't know it but Plaistow years back virtually resembled this arrangement, with Alec Lyle as Refinery Manager under the Refinery Directors. The device in effect divides the top management role into leading and admin. 'As for living,' said Oscar Wilde, 'my servants do that for me.' With the routine looked after, the CE or Army Commander does not have to be all things to all men. One with a vital marketing flair or entrepreneurial talent can exercise this skill to the full while his Chief of Staff keeps the company's management going for him. By this flexibility and this sound allocation of priorities between individuals, in turn relieving the leader of superfluous stress and preoccupation, the effectiveness of the organisation must be enhanced.

There are other ways of helping to skin the workload cat. A Personal Assistant is obviously one. In view of his or her juniority the role demands tact to relieve the CE of much work whereas in the Army the Chief of Staff ranks equally with the corps commanders. A senior person to run 'the chairman's office' can also be beneficial; again the role does not sound half as embracing as the chief of staff's.

The military have played tunes around the staff system theme. Napoleon used Marshal Berthier to handle movements and logistics. The German Army, who originated the complete arrangement, used to have a rule that a chief of staff who dissented from his Army Commander's decision had to report this in writing to the next higher headquarters (interestingly, it was Hitler who rescinded the rule). The mind boggles at a civilian counterpart so I refrain from advocating it, entertaining though it would be, but it does demonstrate how powerful a staff can become. The German scheme could and did supply the higher HQ with an alternative and supplementary information channel as staff officer talked to staff officer and in their case they used it in the Great War to their notable benefit.

In 1914 Germany had 86% of its army invading France and a mere 4 corps screening East Prussia from 9 attacking Russian corps. In the initial actions the Germans came off worst and retreated. Their commander, General von Prittwitz, panicked and telephoned the Chief of the German General Staff, von Moltke, to tell him that the whole of East Prussia – the prized heartland of Germany – must be instantly abandoned. Moltke phoned von Prittwitz's chief of staff, Colonel Hoffman – staff officer talking to staff officer – to have his assessment. Hoffman said that no such retreat was necessary and that the tactical tables might indeed be turned on the enemy. Moltke immediately sacked von Prittwitz and his replacement implemented Hoffman's plan to win the resounding victory of Tannenberg which wholly restored the Germans' stance on their eastern front.

There are lessons here. A commander or senior executive must be able to see the bigger picture and identify the main chance coolly. His boss can benefit from alternative sources of information and tapping these – if needs be by overt or covert by-passing – may be fully justified by results. The new team in the East won credit for Tannenberg when much of it was due to Hoffman. The need to know who did what affects staff assessment and promotion and future organisation . . . but how do you find that out? Not easy! But if you don't or can't the penalty may be painful.

32 Practical Delegation: 'Divisional Directors'

For much of my time we executive directors had each a cluster of units for which we were responsible to the Board, the allocation being more or less suited to individuals' knowledge, abilities (?) and interests. For example, alongside a refinery command my portfolio at one time included Research, the Computer Department and the chairmanship of the Costing Committee, amongst other creatures. In the seventies we were increasingly aware of able senior managers' reasonable and burgeoning ambitions and hence the need to create just below Board level an array of satisfying jobs.

Unsure how to do this without ourselves vanishing from the scene (we didn't think the unthinkable) we had en masse a consultation with Dr Saul Gellerman. Dr Gellerman had 25 years as a consultant, then 15 as Dean of the Graduate School of Management, University of Dallas, and now had his own company – Saul Gellerman and Associates. He had tact, ideas and considerable intellect. Here is an example from his book, *Motivation in the Real World*:

> . . . bad bosses are almost never all bad . . . most bad bosses have an uneven competence profile. They are usually very good in the technical aspects of their jobs, or in tasks that require specialized knowledge or skills. In other words, they are good at doing what their subordinates are supposed to do. They are just not good at managing them. A bad sales manager, for example, probably is (or was) a really super salesperson. A bad engineering manager probably is (or was) an exceptionally capable engineer. Indeed, those strengths were probably the main reasons why bad bosses were selected for managerial jobs in the first place. The problem is that their technical virtuosity tends to blind us to their lack of skill in building and maintaining relationships. The bad boss is a lopsided whose technical wizardry is offset by clumsiness in the motivational part of his job . . .

He led us – we thought we were leading ourselves – to the 'Divisional Director concept' Gellerman used the analogy of a viceroy. The British Government would appoint someone Viceroy of India, telling him to go there for five years and look after it and British interests; on his return at the end of that period they would find out how he had got on. Given sound selection of the satrap and his having the Government's complete confidence, you had appropriate delegation to a satisfied man. It wasn't to be quite like that with us but each of us had a portfolio of profit centres, each with its CE but the relation with him was to be that of facilitator and supporter and mentor rather than that, as hitherto, of boss and subordinate. A CE would thus present his results and plans to the Group CE, Saxon Tate, with his Divisional Director aiding and abetting as they had discussed the plan together before it was presented. The then chairman, Lord Jellicoe, took a keen interest in management succession; sessions on this for each unit with him took the same pattern – CE plus director. It was in fact extremely satisfying to show off to the top brass the quality of one's people and to have it recognised.

If a CE had a decision to make which exceeded his authority and I was not available, he was encouraged to go straight to Saxon, informing me later what was decided. I found the arrangement comfortable and congenial. Perhaps it suited the lazy delegator. It worked less well with more traditional colleagues. Now with more delegation the need and 'empowerment' the cry, controls might be relaxed further. To check on financial misbehaviour with today's reduced moral standards, one could apply the Green remedy; use auditors to supplement the company's own accountants to maintain a discrete surveillance.

Chapter IV

Home Grown Economics

'The meek may inherit the earth – but not its mineral rights.'

– J Paul Getty

33 Arguments for Private Enterprise

Everyone in management is confronted by economic issues: pricing decisions, distribution charges, wage rates, salary structures and political influences on economic matters – through socialism, regulation and so on. On some, finding little help from outside, I thought through some conclusions for myself.

Socialists used to favour state control of private enterprise. One outcome would be replacing private shareholders with a state-run capital allocation system. Instead of paying dividends to investors we would, through taxation, pay for the necessary state bureaucracy. Considering the number of companies in the country, their varied needs and profitability, their competence and prospects, the number of (highly competent) bureaucrats would have to be very large. The resulting expense does not seem on the face of it any less than paying for the stock exchange and investment incomes. It would also inflate dependence on the state, the power of civil servants and the erosion of personal initiative.

Furthermore, capital allocation is now purely by economic judgement – and even then is difficult enough when guided by such limited criteria as the probability of a pleasing pay-off. With the best will in the world the state could not avoid political involvement. I lived through the state steel allocation regime in the fifties. It was exceedingly tiresome, time consuming and inefficient. With a much more complex and extensive task, even performed by bright and knowledgeable and dedicated people, I cannot foresee anything but redoubled incompetence. Visits to post-Gorbachev Russia confirm this. Seventy years of communism with its total state control of economic activity, has left only rusting industries, pollution and impoverishment. Large organisations like Kirov, who made tanks and tractors, and Svetlana, in industrial and consumer goods manufacture, have either no wish to cease being directed and looked after by Moscow or, if they desire a freer life, have no conception of how to make use of it. I have visited both companies. The older order used to tell them what to make, with what and for whom. The current freedom with uncertain suppliers in differing parts of the country to manufacture for unpredictable customers has left them baffled. The Russian scene is no advertisement whatever for socialism.

34 Private Wealth and Public Freedom

Private means, earned or inherited, can provide power and resources to individuals with which to resist the coercion of the state. Inherited wealth, arising by definition from sources outside society's direct control, can confer more or less complete independence of employer or fashion or public opinion. Most rich people will play with their money and waste it although they may by accident create jobs and incomes while doing so.

> It is the business of the wealthy man
> To give employment to the artisan.

If they spend money on consumption they create a demand for goods and services; if they save they create capital for investment. Most will probably not exploit their power to society's advantage but it is latent; some will and do use it. This can benefit the many, not just the few.

A topical example that appeals to me personally, as one who is appalled by Brussels' grotesque mania for increasing control over local matters, was the campaign to modify the centralisation mania of the European Community being waged by Sir James Goldsmith. He was not only organising publicity for his to me very wholesome views but, by financing such test cases as Lord Rees-Mogg's challenge of the legality of the Maastricht Treaty in a British court, is doing what he (and a few others) can do to counter the effective disenfranchisement of the British electorate in the matter of EC membership and conditions.

Here is another example. Nevil Shute describes in his book, *Slide Rule*, his working for a private company building the successful airship R100, while the state built the disastrous R101. After this experience he went on to work for the Admiralty in the War and found that speed required trying to short-circuit the system, persuading reluctant senior officers to cut corners. Whenever he and his colleagues found lively officers needing no prod and eager to get on with the war they predicted he had private means. 'Inevitably investigations proved that we were right'.

Sir James' crusade was of a piece with an ancient tradition. Magna Carta was not screwed out of the autocratic King John by salarymen or by state employees but by stinking rich barons who owned their own castles and could levy armed retainers. With private means politicians or judges or public servants or people able to influence public decisions or taste or fashion can to that extent be independent and do what they feel is right. I know of no other system that can compare with capitalism in this respect. Freedom, like peace, is indivisible. As F A von Hayek says in *The Road to Serfdom*, 'The system of private property is the most important guarantee of freedom, not only for those who own property but scarcely less for those who do not.'

35 Capitalist Attitudes: USA versus UK

We are ambivalent about private enterprise and what the state should provide. I shall decide how to spend my income . . . more money for the NHS . . . private healthcare a growing business. But some countries have a capitalist attitude and the working population automatically approves and makes use of the private enterprise system. Here is an American example. T & L, actually working through the medium of its Canadian subsidiary, rescued an American sugar refinery at Yonkers in New York State from bankruptcy – quite a popular move locally where city employment was involved. When I toured the refinery the recovery programme was well advanced; major reconstruction and reorganisation were yielding reward. A cab from a local company was organised to take me back to Kennedy Airport. This was part of the conversation:

Cab driver: How's the refinery [a large local employer] doing?

CL: All right. It looks like we have an on-going business now.

CD: That turnround's good news.

CL: You seem interested. Do you own this cab company yourself?

CD: No. I wish I did. I'm just a driver. Actually it's owned as to 50% by a Canadian company and 50% by an British company – just as yours is, Mr Lyle!

I wish I could have had – this was in the seventies – such a talk in Britain.

In Russia an instinct for private enterprise has to some extent survived communism. My hotel in St Petersburg was swarming with friendly ladies – in the bars, in the lobbies, in the corridors, everywhere. Some invested roubles to hire a hotel bedroom as a 'honey trap' to earn dollars. The room next to mine was so occupied. There was an insistent knocking on the wall. Later I heard a knock on my door, 'Can I borrow a pencil, please?' Her valedictory comment was that she was there to please . . . Surprisingly the pencil was returned. Clearly privatisation had arrived. But not always attractively. My phone rang at 3 am A warm female voice, 'Are you lonely? Would you like company?' My Russian friends next day told me that if I had said 'Yes', there would have been a knock on the door within minutes – a pretty lady plus boy-friend with a gun. The motive was armed robbery.

But there was not private enterprise everywhere. Gorbachev introduced perestroika – under American pressure, said one Russian to me – but then prohibited alcohol to cure the widespread drunkenness. He allowed his lieutenant, Ligachev, to destroy Crimean vineyards and bottles. As beer and vodka then lacked for bottles, customers queued to collect drink in their own jars.

Although many people in the West practice private capitalism in their own commercial affairs, the capitalists' image is not very handsome. This deserves attention. Michael Ivens, Director of *Aims of Industry* wrote in *The Times*,

Few useful citizens in the history of man have had such ambivalent treatment by society as the capitalist – unless you include the public hangman. The capitalist provides goods, services, employment. .. most of the taxes, innovation and a harnessing of science and industrial development for human desires and needs. What more can he do to achieve saintliness?

36 The Concept of 'Needed Profit'

I think the private enterprise system lacks explanation and is insufficiently understood, which makes for needless conflict in industry. The case for it – which I believe is a strong one – is often going by default. It is simply not being put over. Here is an example of an important mutual understanding.

Tate & Lyle's UK refining business was and is performed by a subsidiary company. When I was responsible for this unit the impact of the EEC, by cutting off a third of our raw sugar supplies, raised costs seriously and reduced profits to below 4% on sales, which was far too little to finance what would now be called our re-engineering. A severe and painful retrenchment and reconstruction campaign affecting everyone in the company was called for. To design and prepare for the acceptance and implementation of this programme we held informative and consultative meetings with all staff, the final one being a large session at a Heathrow hotel with trade union representatives – general workers, electricians, engineers, the lot – some fifty in all from all over the company. We made a thorough and frank presentation, the 'keynote address' at the end being my lot, before the consultation began.

Our trading profit, I pointed out, was then (in the early seventies) about £3 ½ million a year – in a shop steward's eye 700 times his own annual wage. I said we had to have a certain profit surplus if we were to be sure of maintaining a continuing business and employment. How much had this surplus to be? There would or should be the following calls on it:

Financing expenditure on the renewal of sugar refinery plant not covered by our provisions for depreciation (considerably due to inflation).

Paying dividends to maintain the working capital provided to us by shareholders and used to finance stocks, wages, etc. before sales revenue is received (this was actually done by the parent company but we had to contribute our share to that).

Paying the parent for certain central services – government and investor relations, treasury and personnel services, etc – we would otherwise have had to do (more expensively) for ourselves.

Financing some alternative business development as a source of profit and employment to offset the predictable shrinking of the traditional sugar business.

Meeting H M Bloodsucker's demands for tax on our profits.

The presented arithmetic and assumptions on this basis dictated a trading profit of some £7 million a year, or TWICE our current rate. Without this surplus we simply could not be sure we could survive on our present scale. This whole argument stimulated NO critical comment whatever, either in formal session or over the beer later.

It seemed to me that other companies were simply not thinking through and explaining what resources they required for some very wholesome and very necessary purposes, and that they were ignoring trade unionists' complete ability to follow an argument which seriously affected their members' livelihood; they were thus in the process of leaving the word 'profits' as a dirty word in the public's throat. *Profit is needed for survival* – often more than is thought by a trade unionist as reasonable, often less than is commonly thought as actually earned. There is the further point that the reasoning is apolitical and applies equally to public as well as to private enterprise: a nationalised industry must produce some 'surplus' of revenue over cost if it is to meet its financial obligations and to survive.

37 The Public Perception of Profit

I believe the general view of 'profit' – a grossly inflated one – is based on abysmal ignorance, which is very inadequately diluted by managerial effort. Presentation is all. To restore confidence in private enterprise I suggest that 'profit' needs setting in perspective. In no particular order we can do several useful things: redefine the profit objective; state the 'needed profit' level; show where the money does not go.

I fear that few people realise that trading profits for a typical industry will be doing exceptionally well to exceed 10% on sales and even fewer realise that profit *after tax* for a retailer often accounts only for 3p out of every 100p paid for his goods. Furthermore, such figures since the war have been inflated by currency debauchery. Chairmen of companies proudly announce a profit rise of $x\%$ when in real terms in an average year the result is often to remain standing still after adjusting for inflation. Their con trick is misleading themselves and misguiding the public.

Such false impressions are additionally reinforced by loose talk. A car dealer is said to make 17% on a new car when what is meant is that that is the margin to cover all his expenses – barring those met by servicing and used car sales – as well as his trading profit. And this margin needs further qualification. How many cars will he sell in a recession? How long does he have to wait to receive payments? What of bad debts? Does he suffer from thefts and dishonest customers? His reported profit will reflect such factors but only over the long term will reports reveal all his risks. I employ a small-time local plumber as he's pleasant, does good work and his small staff are congenial. Last year his bad debts amounted to £25,000. This is wiping out his business. When I was connected with T & L's UK sugar refining company we had debts outstanding of £8 million – say £90 million in today's money – with only four of our customers.

What real profit is made is not in practice totally siphoned off by greedy shareholders; most is earmarked for prior requirements – hence my emphasising 'needed profit'.

Misconceptions are largely our own fault. There is misleading talk of 'profit' as a company's objective or, more inaccurate still, 'I'm in business to make a profit'.

38 The Profit Objective Fallacy

'I'm in business to make money,' says the Mark I businessman.

'OK. Money just for you?'

'Well, no . . . my staff, my colleagues too.'

'Where does this money come from?'

'Profits.'

'So you are only in business to make a profit?'

To this the company director replies, 'Well, chiefly. I reckon.'

'Oh, really? Why do you want to make a profit?'

'Well, to pay me and amongst other things to reward the shareholders who provide my capital and to finance expansion and improvements and to . . .'

'So these are the concerns you must look after and profit enables you to do so?'

'Yes.'

'You use your profit to fund the development of the company?'

'Yes.'

'Why do you do this?'

'Why? Obviously because it keeps the business going and adapts it to changing conditions.'

'Why keep the business going?'

'To secure my salary.'

'But the company exists separately from you. It will go on after you retire. So why keep it going?'

'To reward my children and to look after the staff, the customers and perhaps help the community generally.'

'How do you ensure you can maintain this to you very necessary cash flow come rain, come shine, in a competitive world and in the long term?'

'Ultimately, I suppose, it boils down to one criterion: if my customers are satisfied everything else follows from that.'

'So customer allegiance is the prime essential for survival?'

'Yes, I suppose so . . .'

'To make money you must survive!'

This seems as far as we can go. Here is the ultimate objective. The company's survival suits everyone: the insiders (employees and owners) have jobs and dividends, they can exercise their skills and make money; meanwhile, the outsiders (customers, the state) obtain needed goods and services, tax revenues and the social benefits of employment. And everyone involved, including all insiders, are also customers. In my book *What The Civilian Manager Isn't Taught* I make this point,

> The purpose of the company, all can say, is to provide useful things. Its prime objective is to serve its customers. It cannot do this nor satisfy the personal objectives of the insiders unless it survives. Thus its continuing objective is simply survival.

Within this overall objective are supportive ones covering the maintenance and improvement of the company. These in turn depend on profitability. Profits underwrite the whole enterprise: they are the *means* to these *ends* . . . This distinction does not affect at all the point that profits are absolutely essential.

They have another use. Other things being equal, profits can measure success and guide investment decisions. Profitability is a simple measuring rod. However, it is still not that which is being measured. Just as a thermometer measures temperature without itself being heat, so profitability measures relative success without itself being the satisfaction of insiders' and outsiders' needs.

The argument is apolitical. A state-owned corporation has or should have the same hierarchy of objectives and needs a 'surplus' (call it profit if you like) over expenses if it is to meet them. It could in the short run be financed by taxation but where in the long run does the tax revenue come from? Answer: from profit, so . . .

39 The Democratic Fallacy

There is continuing pressure to democratise industry, the analogy being between country and a company. The state is run democratically so companies, it is argued, should be also. The European Community (EU) with its social charter wants to thrust works councils down the throats of all larger firms. (It simultaneously eschews such consultation with its own members.) The analogy it and others draw is false. A state's purpose is to maintain and improve the well-being of its inhabitants. If they can contribute to this or, if needful, guide or restrain the government in its behaviour then clearly they should have a say in the process. A company's purpose, its continuing objective, is quite different. It is to serve its customers, not its members. In the process it does the latter of course for every reason – expediency and kindness and to attract the right mix of skills – but this is incidental: the caring supports the pursuit of the objective without itself being it.

There is a better case for customer, not employee, 'government'. *All* organisations have 'customers' of one sort or another and exist to serve them. These people or organisations could with some logic have a place in corporate governance. This should in theory occur through the market place – the customer either buys your product or she shops elsewhere. In practice imperfections in the market dilute this influence. This weakness is made good to some extent by institutions like consumer associations. Though this is only a partial remedy, to attempt more direct 'government' by customers sounds much more difficult than for shareholders, themselves a relatively compact and united body. And these, even when institutions and not individuals, are conspicuously unsuccessful in influencing Boards.

40 Value Added: Use and Misuse

Value Added nowadays is bandied about very freely. Every schoolboy knows about it. (I'm stealing from Lord Macaulay, 'Every schoolboy knows who killed Montezuma and who strangled Atahualpa.') Value Added – sometimes called Net Output – is total revenue less all external expenditure – on raw materials, outside contractors, suppliers of goods and services – that is, all payments to *outsiders*. This sum equals total internal expenditure. VA thus finances all payments to *insiders*:

$$
\left.
\begin{array}{l}
\left.
\begin{array}{l}
\text{depreciation} \\
\text{allocation to reserves} \\
\text{dividends to shareholders} \\
\text{tax}
\end{array}
\right\} = \text{Gross Profit} \\[2em]
\left.
\begin{array}{l}
\text{wages} \\
\text{salaries} \\
\text{bonus payments}
\end{array}
\right\} = \text{employee remuneration}
\end{array}
\right\} = \text{Value Added}
$$

As Robert Heller puts it in *The Business of Wining*,

Added Value . . . stands for a pool of wealth from which everybody involved in the operation has to be recompensed: labour, providers of capital, owners, government.

It may be observed in passing that VAT (Value Added Tax – in the UK £17.5 for every £100 of added value) is an additional levy on profits and wages when both are already taxed individually!

For Government to bleed out more tax, for employees to improve pay and benefits over and above inflation, for management to fund growth and improvement, for shareholders to find capital increasingly rewarded, the VA should constantly increase in real terms. It will be noted that the only group missing from this list of potential beneficiaries is the customer. He has to rely on competition to give reliably to him increasing value for money, even though his satisfaction, as we saw above, is or should be a company's continuing objective.

Some commentators propose the ratio of profit to VA (Profit/VA) or VA per pound of wages (VA/wages) as measures of efficiency when these formulae merely look at the *division* of the 'cake', not at its maximising which is a much more valuable exercise. Now the share of Capital or Labour in the VA is important for corporate health but the insiders – and these are the people we are currently talking about – want or should want as their first priority to increase its size and only after that discuss changes in its allocation (trade unionists usually pass by this benefit for their members). VA is increased by raising sales revenue – by more and better products commanding higher prices, and/or by reducing costs for the same output – saving energy, ingredients, outside contractors' bills and other external expenses.

Question: How much VA is enough or constitutes good
    performance?

Answer: Enough to fund 'needed profit' and employees' satisfactory remuneration.

41 The Division of the Value Added between Capital and Labour

I think it was the economist, Kalecki, who propounded a theorem that the share of profit or wages in the Value Added (VA) is a constant for any organisation. In T & L, for example, the total of wages and salaries was around 63% of the Value Added from 1937 to the late fifties. Thereafter it increased somewhat, reflecting union power and employers' reluctance to risk a strike when – as in T & L's case – selling into hungry markets was easy. Why the constancy? The total of wages is numbers times the average wage. Over time rates increase by more than inflation as standards of living rise, while the number employed falls due to increased productivity. Numbers fall but the cost of each person rises. This broadly offsets the trend to increasing capitalisation through investment, and anyway capital becomes relatively cheaper over the years. Thus unit costs change but the *ratio* of total capital investment to total wages remains steady.

The implications of this are entertaining. The net result of all the annual wage haggling and trade union activity has been to keep Labour's share of the 'cake' constant! Then why not skip all the aggro and pay that steady percentage of the VA – 63% or whatever – into a Wage Fund, each person getting out of it an amount governed by job evaluation and total numbers employed? Thus productivity improvements would *automatically* generate wage rises amongst those employees remaining. Annual arguments (and trade unions?) would be superfluous. It would be readily perceived by employees that a strike must reduce the VA, so must reduce wages. The Scanlon Plan is one of several similar schemes to work on this system. I talked to employees at one such factory and their attitude coincided with this perception I have sketched.

Trade unions appear not to realise that their efforts have only reflected natural processes. Indeed, by strikes and resisting automation, they have reduced the size of the 'cake' while seeking to increase their share of it. (Conversely, their resisting any reduction in wage rates in recent years has thrown the burden of the recession onto those made redundant. It is the unemployed who pay for rigid wage rates.) It follows that a policy of badgering managements or collaborating with them, as appropriate, to improve efficiency, could have raised earnings in Britain *severalfold.* If I had been a trade union member I would have asked the union, 'Why can't I have my wages doubled so that mine can compare fairly with rates across the Atlantic?'

In the sixties I said to Plaistow's Personnel Manager: 'We now employ some 2000 people in the refinery. If, after allowing for differing outputs and product mix, we equalled the productivity of T & L's refinery in Canada, how many people would we have?' After several weeks he returned with the answer, 'About 700.' Dividing much the same 'cake' – the two plants worked very similar process equipment – amongst a third of the number of employees would have boosted wages interestingly.

There would have been attractive side-effects. Overheads like payroll preparation would have been saved. Managers' work would have been enormously simplified and they would have had the time and scope for giving their staff individual attention. In return for high wage rates they could have demanded high performance. They could also have been attractive employers and able to pick and choose their staff. These by-products of high productivity would all in turn have boosted Added Value and further improved productivity – a beneficent spiral. I regret to admit that we never in my time really pursued this enticing prize.

42 Value Added a Measure of Efficiency?

Are there useful tests of performance involving VA? In economic terms success connotes a high 'output' relative to 'input'. We saw in section 39 that a 'high enough' VA is one covering at least the sum of Needed Profit plus superior or competitive wage rates. The resources monopolised in generating this VA are the capital and labour employed in the business. Capital Employed is a conventional accounting figure. Labour Employed is the sum of the number of people at each level of skill times the wage or salary at each level averaged, one presumes, over the country. I cannot see this bit of arithmetic commanding much authority although the idea appears in a 'human resources audit'. More illuminating may be an inventory of 'intellectual capital'. Thomas A Stewart in *Fortune* magazine writes:

> Bates [an advertising agent] ... saying that intellectual capital comprises human capital (talent), structural capital (knowledge artefacts like intellectual property, methodologies, and software), and customer capital (client relationships). Every company has all three, but emphases differ. A three-star restaurant emphasises the chef's human capital; Burger King relies on the structural capital of recipes and processes; a local diner thrives thanks to customer capital – the waitress who calls you 'Hon' and knows you like your coffee with milk, no sugar.

If a company's external payments were less than its competitors for the same sales revenue this would boost its VA and denote efficient cost control. Thus revenue per pound of VA (sales % VA) has some meaning. Equally, very attractive products commanding higher prices for average costs would similarly show up in this measure.

Remuneration as a fraction of VA reflects the degree of capitalisation, other things being equal. Either way, it appears rather uninformative.

The United States is keen on two variants of VA. One is the Economic Value Added (EVA) which is defined as net profit after tax less the cost of total capital employed. The latter goes beyond the accountants' definition and includes all capital, for which some (dubious?) estimating is needed. Nevertheless, however qualified, a negative value which some companies disclose must make one sit up and think. The second measure is the Market Value Added (MVA) and is the market price of invested capital less the cost of shareholders' capital plus bonds plus loans plus retained earnings. If positive this means management has created perceived wealth. *Fortune* magazine points out that EVA measures last year's performance while MVA assesses future prospects. Both would therefore seem to have their uses.

There are of course non-VA based financial ratios, on which I have no worthwhile comment. In T & L's sugar business looking at physical measures rather than or as a support to financial ones extended high up into the organisation. Export tonnages, sugar yields and losses, energy consumption, packeting efficiencies – such figures were the stuff of refinery control. Similar aids must apply in many industries.

43 An Efficiency Improvement Target

Private enterprise has been supremely successful at generating wealth. The UK's real income per head increased by about 1¼% per year at compound interest over eight decades. This may sound modest but actually it meant income per head more than doubled between 1875 and 1960. Performance has fluctuated since then and sometimes beaten the long haul figure. If we can now average a growth of 2% pa., then by 'the rule of 72' (this formula for impressing our fellows with our lightning mental arithmetic says that x% compounded per annum means the value is doubled every $72 \div x$ years) we double income every thirty-six years. Not bad.

Manufacturing industry should be a substantial contributor in this endeavour. (Of course services now weigh in with an increasing proportion of the country's wealth but stimulating manufacturing can only magnify it further while itself offering to diversify the economy and to widen the opportunities for employment open to more types of skill.) For an individual company this means it can expect national wages to rise by 2% per annum in real terms. Pre-war, the rise in prosperity took the form of falling prices, as we saw earlier but that way of doing things is unfashionable now. If the company cannot match this wage rise it will lose skilled people and manpower. It can finance the wage rise either by reducing numbers employed for the same VA and sales revenue or by saving external expenses or by some combination of the two. It *could* raise prices but that deprives consumers of their share in increased prosperity as well as threatening competitive power, so is neither a safe nor a long term solution. The firm must also raise trading profit by 2% per annum to finance dividend increases, taxes and capital expenditure – the extra wealth should not just go to Labour. Anyway, the community wants its share too though the taxman may not phrase it quite like that in his tax demands.

It follows that the target improvement for the average firm is 2% extra VA per annum, modified by any labour and capital productivity increases achieved. A major source for such improvement can be the renewal of obsolete plant and equipment and processes and their replacement with the modern improved equivalents. In a sugar refinery this procedure was a major and continuing one, costly in managers' time and company money. Proposals put forward were quite often for renewing old plant when the new offered only marginal performance improvement. The case for this unrewarding expenditure, and also for proceeding with the opposite – the seemingly premature replacement of a young plant with a much better one, caused much debate in T & L. Why and when should we renew our physical assets?

44 The Timing of Renewals Expenditure

The plant or process we have is ageing – joints and glands are leaking, bearings are worn, technique is outmoded, capacity is ill-matched to throughput. As time passes the resulting extra costs over those for a brand new plant rise still further. Meanwhile new and better plant is becoming available through R & D, which is (or should be) also offering a better cheaper process. When the current costs sufficiently exceed those for a new plant, it pays to scrap the old and install the new. The following diagram illustrates this process. The top line represents sales income, assumed for simplicity to be constant. The saw-tooth lines illustrate total operating costs for two renewal policies – renewing every n or every 2n years. The diagonal line represents 'ideal costs' – those we could achieve were we to have the latest and best equipment at any one time; for simplicity this again is taken to be a straight line when in practice it too would be saw-toothed as R & D breakthroughs occur intermittently.

By renewing we can approximate to the ideal line more or less closely. At year n plant A starts up and works at minimum costs. With time these diverge from the norm, even more so from the ideal. At year 2n we renew and costs drop to the then available minimum.

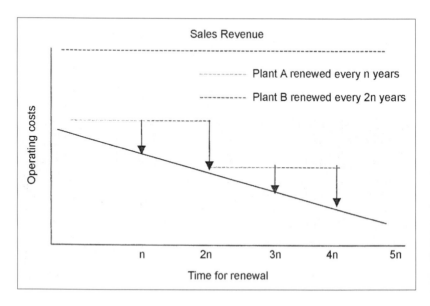

With plant B we delay renewal until it is 3n years old. Which interval pays best?

This all depends . . . on the rate of actual cost deterioration, on the rate of innovation and on the cost of capital, but some general points apply.

At year n we are at ideal cost with a brand new plant so obviously instant demolition and replacement (except with Hong Kong high-rise blocks!) would waste money. Neglecting capital charges, savings % replace cost are zero. After n years costs will have diverged increasingly from best practice until at year 2n we reach break-even point, when we are as well off with the new plant as with the old – that is, total new costs equal total old. Looking at that plant in isolation and ignoring competing claims for capital, at that point we should renew. Delay beyond year 2n would increase the *percent return*, assuming no inflation, but is not meritorious because it is only procured by incurring a further increase in running costs. This is equivalent to lying on a bed of nails to have the pleasure of getting off it.

The precise timing of a renewal can be determined by estimating the Discounted Cash Flow (DCF) rate of return at intervals until it reaches the break-even point or the target rate of return for the particular company. DCF should be used as it introduces into the calculation an allowance for the timing of the incidence of expenditure and savings over the foreseeable future. The replacement cost will be incurred tomorrow but the savings will only accrue the day after and the day after that and a pound today is worth more than a pound tomorrow. (T & L introduced DCF analysis for investment decisions in the sixties. *The Times* as recently as July 1994 quotes a CBI study. 'Researchers found that 68 per cent that replied [to the survey] favoured a simple payback method to evaluate investment proposals'. Comment seems superfluous.)

As a generalisation I look at the break-even return like this. Assume a plant has reached the end of its estimated economic life;

its depreciation charge can be zero. The cash accumulated by way of depreciation over its life and available to fund its renewal is earning interest at say i% pa. The running cost of the old plant is e_1% replace cost pa. After renewal the cash in hand is spent and the interest on it becomes zero. Depreciation on the new plant is d% replace cost pa – I assume the old and new plants cost the same for simplicity – and its running cost is e_2% replace cost pa. Clearly to break even we have:

$$\text{net old expenses} = \text{net new expenses}$$

$$e_1 - i = e_2 + d$$

Therefore the saving in running costs $= e_1 - e_2 = d + i$.

So if we are to be no worse off after renewal the savings must show a return on capital expenditure at least equal to the depreciation and interest rates: that is, a return for a typical firm working on a 25 year plant life of $4 + $ say 10% or so. To allow for optimism on savings and capital costs a cut-off of perhaps 20% (or the equivalent in DCF terms) may well be realistic.

In practice there are good and bad reasons for neglecting profitability. The former come in several forms: the old plant may contaminate the environment or be dangerous or too unpleasant to operate; alternatively, governments, particularly the Brussels bureaucrats, may legislate on operating standards or simply want standardisation for its own sake. A poor reason to accept an inferior return is the absence of a better modern equivalent. T & L's refineries had one process involving massive plant which was difficult to improve by development work more than superficially; age forced replacement at quite inadequate returns.

My graph showed the ideal cost line perpetually improving: were it to flatten out for several years renewals should be drastically postponed – if the far-sighted design of the plant permits of adequate maintenance, supported if needs be by piecemeal renewal of constituent parts.

It has been said in defence of low returns that all the easy savings have been made. If you have halved your work-force over the years it is hard to maintain the same rate of productivity improvement. This argument ignores the fact that each person remaining is paid much more than before so a smaller percent improvement yields the same (worthwhile) saving.

Another conclusion arising from modern renewal theory conflicts sharply with the popular view. Suppose as Minister for Defence you are planning to re-equip the RAF's fighter force. A British company has spent millions developing its design to meet your specification; there are foreign designs competing for the business, most cheaper than the British. Surely, says the person in the street, you must take into account all that the country has spent before you get dazzled by the imported version's apparent savings? The answer is, No. The past expenditure is spilt milk. The only thing within your power is to minimise expenditure from *this* day forward and the design that does that is the winner – neglecting of course all the non-financial reasons for buying British, which may well be weighty. T & L spent big money re-equipping its boiler plant to burn cheap coal. Not long after, another change in equipment and fuel prices offered a handsome enough return to justify immediate expenditure. The apparent waste of recently spent cash which delayed renewal might avoid – as it seemed to the Board – threatened the loss of valuable savings.

45 Investment: When? How much?

T & L switched from a simple pay-back period or return on investment to Discounted Cash Flow (DCF) as a way of allocating surplus profit between competing projects for investment. This is based on the simple premise that a pound today is worth more in your pocket than a pound tomorrow. Everyone knows that, but does one know by how much?

Suppose a project earns cost savings or profits of £100,000 per year in present money and that competing investments earn 10% a year. If this one, a two-year one, starts to earn in the 3rd year, the extra contribution will only be worth £75,000 by then in terms of present money and will total £441,000 over 10 years from now, i.e. 7 years' earnings. If completion were delayed one year, the total contribution is £366,000 – 17% less.

This shows us that investments should be made to start paying off as quickly as possible, that project speediness is very valuable, and that comparison of competing projects' income streams as to amount and timing is essential to make choice authoritative. All straightforward? An unemotive discipline to be adopted forthwith by your Capital Expenditure Committee? Not a bit of it ... My proposal caused argument. One of T & L's most senior directors, Peter Runge, said to me, 'I don't like this approach ... I'm not in favour of defensive strategies, I prefer making sallies from the citadel ...' In the end a balanced view was taken.

Using DCF makes for rational decision-making provided the input data is valid. In a big project, say a new factory, future costs may go awry. Older plant will give trouble, lose output, be overtaken by legislation. Income streams from product sales may be wildly optimistic. Garbage in = garbage out.

Here is a real life example of investment bungling. My little company (see Chapter V) has extensive dealings with a chemical company turned food firm. The decision for them was, should they invest management time and advertising money (both revenue, not capital expenditures) in marketing our product in the UK? On their reckoning they could make a margin of some £400/tonne or 20% on sales which, on forecast sales of perhaps 1,000 tonnes pa. to start with, might leave them with little profit after promotional costs. (Their distribution and other costs were excessive in our view but this they disregarded. Being an ex-chemical firm they aimed for a margin of 50% to cover high fixed costs – which were not applicable in our case.) If the profit were really small the decision not to go ahead was correct.

However, they could have worked closely with us, used our name and methods, concentrated on rifled advertising in place of a dear shot-gun approach, and been content with much lower sales on a higher gross margin. On sales of say 300 tonnes pa. they might have made a mere £100,000 pa initially with prospects of growth. Their sum should have been this – how much do we make if we do this modest latter scheme *compared with doing nothing?* The answer? £100,000 less zilch = £100,000 pa. As this profit should grow as the market became worked over, as their own product on their own admission had declining consumer appeal, they had the opportunity to make something instead of nothing as well as obeying the dictum that if you are losing market share then lose it to your own product and thus: (1) make *extra* money (2) preserve your market presence (3) pre-empt the competition (4) demonstrate enterprise to your shareholders.

46 How to Maximise your Pay

The pool of free money available to pay wages and salaries is included in what economists call the Value Added (VA) or Net Output. This, as we have seen, is total expenditure on everything less payments to 'outsiders' – suppliers, contractors, etc., all in fact who are not personally involved with the company as investors or employees. Put another way, it is the sum of wages, salaries, and trading profits. Often profits take 20% to 50% of the VA, employees the rest. The division follows their relative contributions. If everything is automated and worked by few people, the shareholders will have contributed the most by buying all this equipment. They will then take the lion's share. T & L had a lighterage business – some cheap barges worked by many men – where Labour's share of the VA was 99%.

Thus each 'average' person receives Labour's overall share of the VA, the cake which all share, divided by the number of employees. So the rules for high pay are simple:

- Choose a company that is very efficient and successful – to make the VA as big a possible.

- Work skilfully so that employees are few in number.

- Don't let trade unions try to increase Labour's share of the cake at the expense of reducing its size: this is unlikely to pay! Better to work with the management to maximise the size of the cake.

47 A Summary: Economics and Politics!

Here, with succinct pungency, is a convenient synopsis of highly conventional wisdom to guide our thinking and voting. The title is 'Cow Politics':*

Feudalism You have two cows. Your lord takes some of the milk.

Pure Communism You have two cows. Your neighbours help you take care of them, and you all share the milk.

Applied Communism You have two cows. You have to take care of them, but the government takes all the milk.

Dictatorship You have two cows. The government takes both and shoots you.

Singaporean Democracy You have two cows. The government fines you for keeping two unlicensed farm animals in an apartment.

---

*Reproduced from *Global Village – a weekly posting from cyberspace* in *The Times Weekly*.

Pure Democracy You have two cows. Your neighbours decide who gets the milk.

Representative Democracy You have two cows. Your neighbours pick someone who will tell you who gets the milk.

Capitalism You have two cows. You sell one and buy a bull. Your herd multiplies, and the economy grows. You retire on the income.

Totalitarianism You have two cows. The government takes them and denies they existed. Milk is banned.

European Democracy You have two cows. The government regulates when you can milk them. Then it pays you not to, takes both, shoots one, milks the other and pours the milk away. It requires you to fill in a form accounting for the missing cows.

Chapter V

Starting Your Own Business

'It is a quietness in a man's mind to live upon his own and
know his heir certain.'

– Prof. R H Tawney

48 A Case Study: Lyle Foods

Here is what can actually happen. I left T & L in 1982 with the idea
that intense sweeteners (IS) such as saccharin or aspartame or
T & L's own one – Sucralose – should not be marketed by a food
company as a pill, even though it minimised calorie content, as being
too chemical, too simply copied, and aligned to retail only through
pharmacies. Instead, a good IS should and could be formulated into
a food, even if calories were not minimised, and to be branded by a
food company and sold through food retail outlets. Thus the *product
concept*.

I was out of a job so I wanted to use my energies and knowledge
and create an inheritance for my family. T & L had been a family
business but, having become a public one, had succumbed to City
pressures and professional managers. Lacking a controlling

shareholding and perhaps sufficient managerial talent, we had in an evil hour (for the family, if not necessarily for the shareholders) appointed a non-family chairman, George Jellicoe, with all that that implied in the way the company was to be run. Jellicoe was very able – intelligent, an accomplished conceptual thinker, replete with useful contacts in the outside world, personable, humorous, dutiful – *but* a politician, not primarily a manager. He felt free to manipulate people in contrast to the firm's tradition of mateyness, team spirit and morality. No doubt many companies are now run that way and increasingly impersonally – not for them a whiff of paternalism while sometimes simultaneously demanding staff loyalty. Let that be. *My* company was going to be and remain a family one.

A consultancy with a US sugar company, whose CEO was a friend (a useful *contact*, italicised words subject of an expanded discussion later) enabled me to explore the idea in practice, using his food technologist and marketing man to assess *market acceptance.* The product we devised was simple – just IS and sugar to give half the bulk, half the calories for the same sweetness as sugar. (British Sugar now sells this type under the brand name *Half Spoon* and at a premium over sugar of up to 67%.) The market research company reported glowingly – 'a unique public response!'. We went to market. Sales were disappointing. There seemed to be a lesson in this.

More thought. Trouble was the product was nothing special, just lowish calories. Now what about using a bulking agent in a clever way to make it look like sugar? If this were achieved, what sort of company would be required to exploit it? Big or little? I thought, a little one, which would be flexible, suited to serving a niche market and to my limited means. I talked to my ex-employer, Neil Shaw (now Sir Neil) and we agreed it was a sort of cookshop operation and unsuited to a large scale processor such as a major refiner. A different *contact* from T & L lead me to a technical man – try such-and-such a process. A chance enquiry lead me to a processing company in Yorkshire. Months of trial and error – then eureka! We had devised a patentable process for making a sugar lookalike – having crunch, taste, versatility, spoon for spooness – all with half the calories of sugar for the same bulk and sweetness. No arithmetic for consumers – use as sugar; family suspicious? No, looks like sugar. Giving up sugar? OK, try this ... better than artificial sweeteners. Don't like sweeteners? OK, this is sugary ... still healthy-looking (there's to be a brown version too) and all part of a modem life style.

We had an attractive product distinguishable from others, to be made by a patentable process. So far our very modest internal resources of people and money sufficed. Chance contacts with a sales agent got us into Tesco and later Sainsbury and Waitrose. Our product *Slite*® was selling. Then the supermarkets wanted promotional support while we had no more resources. We went to a merchant bank who gave marginal help only. They paid a head hunter to *recruit* us a CEO to strengthen the management with practical sugar marketing experience as well as with up-to-date knowledge of current practice. Mostly from friends of friends we raised £460,000. Too late. By then the supermarkets felt disenchanted and delisted us. Our new CEO helped hugely but the family had to accommodate itself to someone, however able and loyal, with a different background and his own objectives.

Back to the drawing board. I won't bore you with much intervening affairs – as Sam Goldwyn said, 'we've all passed a lot of water since then'. We talked to possible allies while exploring doing our own thing, with contracted-out production and packeting, without success. Then a well known company, Monsanto, approached us quite unsolicited. Our product looked to have more long-term life and health than theirs – the sweetener Canderel. They would like to market ours under their name and brand. Fine. A year and a half later we are still talking to *big companies* ... rich in prospects tomorrow but lacking jam today.

Rushing towards the end of the runway, engines roaring, we strive for take-off. At this enthralling moment my story ends. Though cut off, it shows what can happen and what is critical for success.

49 Critical Factors

This simple tale has lessons. First, what sort of a business do you, the creator, want to construct? Large or small? A quickie – a dot com? Making something or just making money? An inheritance to be nurtured and preserved? A one-man/woman band? A consultancy to teach rather than to do? Capital intensive? The choice will affect staffing, funding, operations, the lot . . . It may well be hard to formulate at the outset any precise answer. I had at first only a general idea and that proved to be quite wrong.

Now the *product concept* . . . Pundits say, do not invent a product and then search for a market. First identify a consumer need . . . but searching for a niche to fill presupposes at least some idea of what you can produce. I knew how to make a low calorie sugary product. Much later the market was identified as those sugar users forsaking it for perceived health reasons (which represent a steady drain on a refiner's market share) plus those thinking about doing so plus those who had forsaken it and might be wooed back, perhaps because they were becoming disenchanted with the available low calorie sweeteners – being chemical-seeming or without texture or with an after-taste. In total these items could be perhaps 2% of the domestic sugar market – barely noticeable! – yet adding up to 3500 tonnes a year which, at a target margin of £400/tonne, produces a 'contribution' to overhead and profit of £1,400,000 a year – and this excluding Europe and the Americas. Not to be despised!

Thus more thought and research on *market acceptance* has produced a much clearer market concept as well as a measure of the scale of the operation.

The product creation was helped by having technical advice. This arose on chance *contacts*. The processing technique we use is not esoteric but few sugar refiners are familiar with it so my help came from outside. The moral of the story is this: the network of contacts you build up while in employment can be a rich source of later help. This you may freely tap. You would help them if the roles were reversed.

The *recruiting* you may need to do can supplement what you bring to the commercial party. In Lyle Foods' case, I have sufficient production and technical knowhow to devise a sugary product, to calculate the specification needed to accord with claims of e.g. sweetness and caloric content, and to interrogate our production contractor. I am out-of-date on standards, hygiene and employment legislation to name but a few lacunae! Being ignorant of these is a subtle danger. Your worst problems are the ones you haven't identified.

The selection process must be as rigorous as time allows. Have an open mind on any aid – handwriting, psychological insight, whatever ... Do not neglect references as needless or *infra dig.* The management consultant Anne Shaw told me 30 years ago that she always asked recruits what salary they had received and could she check this with the previous employer, 'You'd be surprised how often this triggered a disclaimer: well, that figure including a special bonus ... so' With three decades of declining standards, what price honesty now?

Then there is a related but less obvious concern. What sort of person are you getting? For all the apparent competence and track record, what's inside? Unscrupulous? Economical with the truth? Overambitious? A plain double-dealer? (Conversely, there may be hidden talents and contacts.) I know examples. Years ago, T & L thought it needed an executive director resident in North America to watch over the company's then modest investments there. Would I consider being this? Yes, I would. A tour there followed and informal friendly talk with local seniors, one then running a biggish operation of ours. He was all friendliness at first but later decided he wanted the job for himself and secretly manoeuvred me out of the running. Not a terrible crime but an unknown type of behaviour at that time.

And seniors can make asses of themselves in the simplest ways. When Neil Shaw became CEO, he wanted very sensibly to warn everyone he meant business and that hard action was needed to improve the company's performance which at that time (and since!!) was lamentable in City eyes. He ordered that all should fly economy class. As mentioned above, I flew to Toronto for a local Board meeting and emerged from the rear of the aircraft only to meet Neil and our Finance Director coming out of the First Class. Neil had also told a journalist that he had cleared out the Rolls-Royces and replaced them with Fords. A fine gesture . . . new broom clearly sweeping clean . . . out with the old and the wasteful . . . There was only one snag. There were no Rolls to eject.

Here was an able man acting falsely and readily to be exposed as such. Shades of Al Gore. They were not great incidents but the internal effect was to undermine the crusade he rightly wanted to endow. His word became suspect, not unfairly.

It reminds me of a great American friend who worked for Johnson & Johnson and later had his own business, initially working on Wall Street. A mutual friend told me that the honourable Wally Steinberg could not do well there because he was dealing with people who could say: 'My word is my bond . . . today.'

My little company has dealt with big ones. This has been enlightening. The supermarkets appear to this outsider remarkably bureaucratic. Possible collaborators – to whom a new product with which to fight clearly foreseeable competition must (you'd be forgiven for thinking) be very welcome – can be painfully slow in reacting and extraordinarily obtuse in their conceptual thinking. This is not sour commercial grapes. They may be unable to appreciate what business they are in and to distinguish between the tactical and the strategic. It should not be that hard to identify which are means and which ends but they can manage to make it hard.

One must muster patience. Repetition and persistence can wear down resistance. Presentation can be varied. One can also avoid being put off by thinking 'they must have thought of that'. You've only just thought of it! Accepting the obvious – *after* it's revealed – as granted is a respectable disease. The US Patent Office says an invention is not patentable if someone versed in the technique could have thought of the idea. But he didn't and you did! How do you define 'versed'? Anybody versed or only fairly inventive people? The argument is nonsense. Many inventions look obvious – after their creation.

Our possible ally with whom we have been talking for 18 months decided recently not to enter the UK market with our products . . . and for good reasons, carefully thought out. Their brand could be counterproductive and make the cannibalising of their own product a first move. We have just thought of their marketing under our brand. It has market cachet. It suits the product much better than their own image. It refutes their own arguments. It could mean that, instead of earning nothing from this market, they could earn something and build an alternative product line to underwrite their declining one. We were surprised to find they hadn't thought of this (nor had we until very recently) and were much taken with it. But second thoughts prevailed: better to keep heads below the parapet and earn nothing than seize an opportunity with its risk . . .

> There is a tide in the affairs of men,
> Which, taken at the flood, leads on to fortune.
> And we must take the current when it serves,
> Or lose our ventures.

50 The Risk/Reward Matrix

Start-ups may well be skimped for funds. My experience is that this can be dangerous for other than obvious reasons. Lyle Foods has for much of its life been living hand to mouth. As a result it has had to eschew positive actions that could save time (and a pound today is worth more than a pound tomorrow) or provide more options (to avoid the deadly Hobson's Choice) or extend patent coverage (a cash hungry business) or conduct R & D. And these research projects needed doing:

- to reduce production costs (including less obvious wastage).

- to improve product quality (conferring additional consumer benefits).

- to specify applications (e.g. for us identified industrial usages).

- to have the knowledge to confer initiative with the production contractor.

- to extend the product range (often popular with supermarkets).

Proper funding would thus have enabled us simply to perform better, conducting all our managerial functions more effectively in the widest sense.

If seeking external funding, it is tempting to raise only a modicum. 'Let's not saddle ourselves with debt or lose too much shareholding . . .' but unless a margin for contingencies is built in, the end result may be – barring a miracle – a black hole. The rule is, it costs twice what you thought and takes twice as long. So don't be too niggardly. Furthermore, consider raising enough to seize the bigger opportunity as well as the short-term or modest one. In our case, we could currently raise £250K to cover a modest marketing launch with an ally and – optionally – a further £250K. to create our bespoke production and packeting facilities with large cost savings. We might go much further and seek to raise £2 to 5 million to finance a large scale in-house production and marketing business for the whole of the UK. Our decision? We haven't been able to take it yet.

If finance is confining, you will constantly be facing decisions where rewards (often exciting-seeming) must be balanced against risks (often dangerous or catastrophic). Then the propensity for risk-taking of each partner will be influencing debate. If such propensities differ which is not unlikely, you must allow for this. How?

In theory, faced by a decision with good and bad possible outcomes, you should predict the probability of success P and its pay-off S. Call this sum $P \times S$. Repeat for the failure, forecasting its cost, and call that $p \times F$. If PS *much* bigger than pF (to allow for a margin of error in a very uncertain process) you can proceed. But what if 'failure' means catastrophe and the dissolution of your company – thus, very unlikely but disastrous if it happens? Here is a real life example.

In 1916 Admiral Jellicoe (George Jellicoe's father) brought the strong German fleet to battle of the coast of Jutland. The risk/reward balance is revealing. If Jellicoe won, the Allies would survive and could carry on the war little affected. If he lost, the Germans could blockade Britain and the Allies would lose the war in 6 months. If the Germans won, they win the whole war. If they lost, not much harm to them would result. Hence Churchill's celebrated aphorism: Jellicoe was 'the only man on either side who could lose the war in an afternoon'. True. But the converse has gone unnoticed: his opponent could win the war in an afternoon. The recommended strategy for them by the pundits was therefore the 'mini-max' one:

The Germans should maximise their minimum gain – i.e. not be overly concerned with losses if the enemy suffered much more.

The British should minimise their maximum loss – i.e. avoid serious losses even at the expense of not inflicting them.

Both combatants adopted these guides – Jellicoe whole-heartedly and to be criticised for so doing, the Germans partially – they could have risked more in hope of gaining more.

Your company could be like Jellicoe's fleet. You simply cannot afford ultimate disaster, however improbable. But you may well be able to run more risk in search of a big pay-off by having a plausible *timely* contingency plan ready. The timing may be vital. The lead-time to implement the emergency plan will be X weeks or even Y months. You have to be ready to press the button before then.

To be cheerful again, measuring risk may be easy and its extent highly manageable. My wife had an interior design business and wanted retail premises so that an attractive display of furnishings and decorative materials would sell more consulting. She identified premises. Should she sign the leasing contract? We calculated that if four customers a day appeared and each spent (from memory) £25, her fixed costs would be covered. She promptly signed the lease . . . and never looked back.

51 Intelligence

I use the military meaning. Information gathering is dull but capable of decisive results. Here are practical examples:

• We wished to know how much a potential competitor spent on advertising a product. Finding out how little this was enabled us to recommend to a new ally a strategy which suited his purse.

• I heard a rumour that T & L's new intense sweetener had finally gained approval for consumption in the EU. This if correct could affect what we did in the UK. I found confirmation via the Internet from a respectable trade source that this was correct.

• Two of my colleagues briefed a US sugar company on the opportunity we could provide. Background information on competitive products was found on the Internet.

103

- In our case scouting supermarket shelves informs us of market conditions. I spotted in Safeway a new T & L granulated sugar pack selling for 116p/kg when the ordinary paper bag was priced at 55p! We can retail at 109p per sugar equivalent kg. Useful pricing guidance!

Useful information can obviously extend over your whole business. Prior patent rights, trademarks, brand names, the availability of new or alternative ingredients, competitive company ownership, commercial practice in possible new markets – the list is lengthy.

The converse of intelligence is security. We use our own proprietary process. Should we patent it? (We did.) To do so tells everyone broadly how to do it yet intellectual property constitutes a worthy asset in financiers' eyes. In any case, all an enemy has to do to learn what he needs is to suborn a production employee or have his own man be taken on to work there. If you are first in the game you can by deft footwork keep ahead. Possession is nine-tenths . . . etc. Then you are always fighting on ground of your choosing.

Real choice anyway may be illusory. When industrial espionage – in plain English stealing other's property – is no longer thought immoral, every organisation is vulnerable. The spy may be caught but the damage may already be done. This subject is now hugely inflated by hacking on the Internet. More on that later.

52 A New Ally: the Internet

We are all now under pressure to get E-lated. I have no special advice on how best and fully to exploit this universal medium. However, here are some lessons I have learned the hard way.

First and most basic, the equipment. I and my family used to buy our computers from Compatibility Ltd, a small supplier/dealer in Sussex. I guess we pay 10 or 20 or 30% more than buying from a chain or 'direct'. I think it an essential investment. The back-up service is superb from installation through to routine trouble shooting. And the latter is badly needed. I have software troubles of some sort several times a *week*. The hardware gives little trouble but the following problems are routine or everyday ones:

- I cannot connect to my ISP. Repetition nearly always solves this. Most often, it simply says 'An illegal action has been performed' and shuts me down; or it has asked me several times today even when I have been using it non-stop 'You have been inactive for some time: do you want to continue?'

- I tried to sign on once with no success. I repeated for 15 minutes. The screen said something like, 'there is only room for one account holder at a time'. Very curious. There is only one of me. I finally get online and find that a hacker has sent out a score of highly pornographic emails over my email address to people I've never heard of. It took a long time to convince them it was not my doing. I am bound to say that my ISP – AOL – took a relaxed view of my complaint and merely advised me to change my address and password.

- I use an instant messaging system. This frequently disconnects one in the middle of a conversation without one's leave. One has to reboot and start again. If the shut down is too peremptory one has to 'rescan all the files'!

- My messaging system recently went wrong: it would not show messages clearly. The Helpline said, 'Uninstall your [old] system and install the [new] one . . .' There followed many lines on how to do this without losing all data. I managed to install the new version and transferred all the old data I wanted *automatically* without the technical work I had been threatened with!

- Sometimes the screen freezes: nothing works, the mouse can do nothing, action of any sort is zilch. I have to shut down and then have to wait for scanning and restarting.

All PC users have horror stories. The stuff may be modern but it is bloody unreliable. Thank God Bill Gates doesn't make my motor car.

Of course Compatibility cannot help with many of these problems but Helplines are sometimes available. I have spent literally hours on the accumulated total of calls I have made to AOL who are invariably helpful, expert and civil; it remains regrettable that such support is needed. I can get instant help from Compatibility on hardware problems, on aspects like hard disk capacity and usage, new programme installation difficulties – if needs be by a person coming here! The firm's policy is not to sell to anyone more than an hour away so that this service can be provided.

Life is not eased by the notorious obscurity of so-called instruction manuals. And the guides purporting to help us through the gobbledegook are themselves unhelpful. I have a copy of the 400-page *Complete Idiot's Guide to the Internet*. The 'Acquisitions Editor' invites readers thus: 'If you have any comments about this book . . . please send them in.' I had several, covering aspects like omissions, obscurity and so on and wrote accordingly. The response? Nil. It remains baffling that organisations produce literature on how to use their products without testing it on or getting it written by ordinary users like us.

Fighting through a jungle of consumer unfriendliness is still worth it. We, small business though we are, have benefitted considerably from using the Internet. I have no special magic to offer but here are some practical aids.

The whole business of tapping the Internet for the huge and rich supplies of information it houses is based on searching. Sometimes websites are known and can be accessed directly. Often they are not known. Enter the search engine. There are horses for courses. If you can state your needs in a few unambivalent words, then Altavista can be best. It functions rather like a dictionary – a big one. If looser wording is the only option, then Google I find admirable. For example, we wanted to know if a foreign company investing in Lyle Foods would be eligible for the same tax incentives as are enjoyed by UK-based investors in start-up ventures. I asked Google to search for something like: 'UK tax incentives for foreign companies'. Two hours later I was talking on the phone to the Treasury official re-drafting the rules.

A relative newcomer with its own angle is Ask Jeeves. This produces a mix of direct references and lists of sources from other search engines. Regardless of engine, much depends on the wording of the question. For example, in my tax example you may need to have the whole sentence within inverted commas to exclude foreign rulings. Some engines want + signs linking essential keywords. Experiment can give the answer.

Internet security is becoming a live concern. My own small brush with a hacker differs in scale but not perhaps in nature to the recent invasion of Microsoft's systems, which we had thought closely guarded. Computer crime is said to be increasing at an alarming rate as clever criminals spot vulnerable holes in companies' lax armour. Here is Mr Andrew Emmerson writing in *The Times* of 30 November 2000 on the subject,

A web-based business [may soon be] sued for failing to safeguard the data of others . . . Ignorance is no excuse when a computer is hijacked unwittingly . . . Undertakings that handle the money or data of others have a duty of care and trust . . .

He then quotes instances of recent security breaches involving well known firms. He goes on,

. . . it is clear that no due diligence has been exercised in bug-testing these systems . . . traditional testing has been forsaken . . . These e-commerce websites holding customer data online, such as credit card information, are particularly exposed to a claim for compensation if this information is inadequately protected.

Enough said?

53 Research and Development

Start-ups may well (nearly always?) have lousy cash flows for a period, often for an uncomfortably long period and often longer than predicted. There will be a huge temptation to keep afloat, to concentrate on the urgent rather than the important, to work for today and let tomorrow look after itself ('procrastinators of the world, unite! – tomorrow'). R & D may appear tomorrow's concern but may actually be more pressing. Our own statement of R & D needs disclosed near – and medium-term work:

Present Product:

- improve stability for industrial applications

- specify new processing aid requirement

- test alternative intense sweeteners which our customers may prefer.

New Products:

- develop flavoured versions of basic product – e.g. maple, honey

- try fructose base instead of sugar for diabetics

- develop very low calorie variant for sachet usage

- develop vitamin-enriched variants tailored by market.

By the last item hangs a tale. Vitamins are *a good thing*. Everyone knows that. Vitamin C, for example, is excreted if taken in excess (though what constitutes excess may be controversial). Other vits are not. Africans are said to be short of vitamin A so adding that looks worthy but this is now seriously disputed. In all conscience one needs to weigh benefit against risk but the US Food & Drug Administration, much less the media looking for red meat, will not do this. The FDA knows it will be blamed if an additive or drug hurts people. It is very unlikely to be criticised if it withholds approval from a beneficial drug of uncertain effects. The decision tree is obvious. Companies trying to do good within FDA guidelines may – as the Vitamin A example shows – get punished.

If the worst happens it's time for crisis management – and how many small firms are ready for that? The classic example of sound instant remedial action is Johnson & Johnson's dealing with contaminated packs of its drug *Tylenol*. Not that many packs were at risk but the then Chairman of the Board, Jim Clare, insisted on instant wholesale removal and replacement in tamper-proof packs, whatever the cost. Customers responded wholesale to this handsome action and remained loyal J & J customers. I had met Jim Clare earlier – a very impressive man so I was unsurprised by his repute.

54 Choosing a Career

Have you preconceived ideas? From the age of three have you wanted to be a brain surgeon? No? Nor me. So you must choose . . . Here are some aids.

Give yourself a choice. Don't just decide on being Prime Minister or a train driver and have nothing else on the cards. Learn what work jobs entail. Have you been in an office, much less a factory? Have you an idea of the routine, of the scope you may have to contribute to it? (Don't be too overawed by technology. Many a business can be improved by straightforward thought, perhaps after some not too difficult learning.) Remember that standards are relative. An academic plodder, at age 16 my tutor said to me in a kindly way, 'You know, Lyle, mathematics is not for you . . .' Five years later I went to work in the family sugar refinery. I there acquired some repute as a mathematician!

Have you friends or family to give you an insight into what goes on in some particular role or can provide an introduction to it? These can be very valuable. Have you hobbies or interests which are conducted out there in the real world seriously? Have you got paper or practical qualifications that could help? These may be acquired – don't neglect an opportunity to get them. Equally, they may help you get a job but may not help you to keep it!

When applying for a job, remember your priorities. The first one is to get an interview. Once there you have a chance; without it, none! This will usually entail answering an advertisement or a 'cold call'. Either means sending a CV (resumé in North America). I have only two points to make on designing this. Let's illustrate with an example. A woman acquaintance in search of a badly needed new job showed me her CV. It showed her as an experienced and competent installer of telecommunications equipment. I asked her was that what she wanted to do? Yes, it was. Further questioning showed that her background wasn't just technical. Was her ambition really fixed on such work? Had she not got managerial ability? Well, yes. Then would she consider a job that offered managing a project or department that also involved technical work? She asked where was there such a paragon of a job? We rewrote her CV to signal that she was looking to perform technical management. We could show her abilities in the broadest terms that were underwritten by her experience and skills, elucidating these by conceptualising all that she had known and done. We then wanted to hit the reader with an instant broad picture of her. This we did by setting out immediately after her name and address a Profile. It looked like this:

PROFILE   Competent site administrator

               Capable team leader

               Strong team worker

               Ability to work unsupervised

Articulate communicator

Computer literate and good keyboard skills

Very flexible, willing to work at any location, both in this country and abroad Prepared to undertake further training if required

This was followed by a concisely worded list of Achievements, then by a Summary of Experience.

She has been offered a very well paid job by a large US company involving world-wide installation work.

Thus two rules, tease out your total competence and experience in the broadest terms; capture attention at the outset for your complete work needs as matched to your abilities. The next stage is being interviewed – now you can try to get the job. Try to research the job beforehand, if you know something about the firm and what it does, you have shown keenness and an ability to learn. Prior experience can help. My company recruited graduates for management training. Those with 1st class honours degrees were suspect – had they spent their time at university studying and missing out on the intellectual and social and sporting life? A man straight out of university aged 22 might seem bright and eager and adaptable. Another, equally useful-seeming, but having spent a year on VSO or driving across Asia or running a garage in France, could seem much more so. (I recruited the garage runner myself. He turned out to be as useful as I had hoped.) When being interviewed, learn about the company. Are you being asked questions or is he/she talking all the time? Is your respect and interest being aroused? Can you meet potential colleagues or see the work-place? All the information you can gather can help you find the job that commands your respect and which satisfies you. Don't neglect the fact-finding. After all, do you want to avoid that Monday morning feeling or don't you?

55 A Day in the Life of a Shift Manager

What's it like to work in industry? This is what it was like for me.

I'd finished fourteen months training, part day-work, part on shifts, working through every department processing sugar, to learn how they worked. I acted as foreman in each one for a fortnight – which can make you nervous! Now I was to be in charge of a whole shift – 300 people, millions of pounds' worth of equipment and machinery. I felt excited in my clean boilersuit, striding out of my office and feeling important even though, having been a sergeant in the Army, I was used to some responsibility.

I went first to the control laboratory to have a quick overview of events – production rate, white sugar quality, processing standards … nothing untoward, luckily! I then walked to the department taking in raw sugar where it got a first clean up (raw sugar can be dirty with bugs, dirt, much from the ships' hold); had a word with several plant operators, 'How are you ? Sugar awkward today? … Good, fine, see you …' I visit the other three floors – all well. I go to the next department … same again. At the third a problem, the foreman whom I know well, says, 'I'm a man short – can't keep pace quite – can you help?' 'No, I can't – have no spare men now but can ask for a dayworker to be transferred tomorrow.' That's all we can do. I move on.

Back to the lab. A question for me. 'So-and-so not good …' … Me, 'What alternatives have we?' 'We can either do A or B'. I've never met this one before. I haven't the faintest idea what to do. I guess or fudge! [This actually happened to me: I can't remember what I said … I fear it was flannel.]

And so through the routine of the shift. I have to know what is going on, deal with problems the other people can't, get to know my staff and their lives, and learn more as I go along about sugar refining. At the end of the shift, I write up the diary and hand over to my colleague who'll manage the next shift. It's a very satisfying job.

It had personal rewards but also obligations. There can be – there will be – crises in all jobs. A condom is found in a sugar packet. (It happened as mentioned previously, not to me, but in the Tate Refinery. Senior people grappled with that one.) There was another crisis I could not escape. We had two boilers each 50′ high, each burning 6 tonnes of coal an hour normally but one was off for cleaning and survey. One night shift I was doing paper work when my phone rang, 'The grate on No. 2 Boiler has jammed – I can't keep the power going'. The 'grate' meant the mechanical coal feeder to the huge furnace. I replied, 'I'll be right down . . .' I ran to the Boiler House through the Turbine Room (we generated our own power by passing high pressure steam from the boiler – if it was running well! – through a 4500 kwh turbine revolving at high speed). The turbine was already beginning to slow down. Not a happy omen! The Boiler House Foreman and I telephoned all departments for a crash shutdown, to reduce power consumption. I went back to look at the turbine. It had slowed into its 'critical speed' where it was out of balance. It was vibrating so violently the lagging was falling off. I felt a worried bunny. Back to the Boiler House . . . everything to be stopped! But all the stock in process could spoil, could set solid if not stirred. We had only the limited electrical supply from the Grid. How many motors could be kept running on that? I asked the Electrical Foreman for a list. I will omit the detail – the night ended with a silent cold refinery but safe, thanks to its fine crew who responded admirably to the crisis – and a tired Shift Manager . . .

Chapter VI

DIY Management

'If you can keep your head when all about you are losing
theirs, it's just possible you haven't grasped the situation.'

– Jean Kerr

'The gambling known as business looks with austere disfavour
on the business known as gambling.'

– Ambrose Bierce

56 Getting Started

We have to manage Department X, our first assignment. (We will
later move on to other different assignments.) Having begun with no
formal management training the first stage – for me – in any job is
to get to know the broad outline, to feel I can get my arms round it.
Here are some simple questions that can force the disclosure of
pertinent information and guidance, and which often unearth
subsidiary lines of enquiry to be followed up as opportunity and
time, very probably in short supply, permit.

Who is my new boss, if any? There may not be one. Who else do
I have to refer to or defer to? What are my responsibilities and
authority; are they recognised formally or only *de facto?* Who works

for me? How do *they* answer the above questions? Do they recognise my role and have they ever heard of me? Is the department's functioning dependent on their personal relations? What is the actual and formal organisation? They may not coincide. Ian Lyle told me that Plaistow's Laboratory was run before the war by a Chief Chemist who had an Assistant. When Ian returned after the war he found that the Chief Chemist was calling his Assistant 'Sir'.

What is the state of morale? Is there any sense of common purpose? Is the organisation of which we are a part respected? If so, by whom? How do managers rate their respective staffs? And rate in their staffs' eyes? What is the product? What criteria define quality and quantity? If these clash which wins? Are product costs – marginal and total – and profits known? Are they amenable to analysis? Who schedules production, and how? What relationships, if any, exist between us and our customers What supports – staff, boss, other departments – do I have? What, if any, are the department's formal or informal objectives? Are we achieving them?

What time-bombs are known to be or may be ticking? Am I vulnerable to unpleasant surprises? Who is steeped in the department's work, practice and problems and so is available and experienced enough to shoot troubles? Do I have exposed or unguarded flanks? Have I enemies lurking in the undergrowth – a customer or a supplier or a managerial rival or whatever? But in thinking what such a one might do to me, I must remember what General Moltke (quoted here by Professor M van Creveld) said to his aides, '. . . the enemy always seemed to have three alternatives open to him and he usually chose the fourth . . .'

Only time to think and delve may expose answers to some questions. It is tempting, or may be just necessary, to start managing while the process of uncovering all requisite information is still unfinished. Once this happens our visible role as boss may inhibit responses to sensitive questions. But that's life. The intelligence gathering will come from discreet surveillance, inferential thinking, open ears, contrived testing of staff.

All this may sound elementary in the extreme. It is meant to be just that. The CEO of Nestle, Helmut Maucher, quoted in the *Director* puts the matter this way.

> Do the normal, sensible thing first. Produce marketable products; look after your management, personnel and customers; check the till. In short, do the obvious: get back to the basics.

Sound advice, and as applicable to a departmental manager as to a CEO.

57 Priorities: 'Critical Areas'

It is enormously helpful to know what activities demand your personal attention and what can be delegated or safely left to the department's routine. What special tasks must *you* do this period because no one else can or should? People below you will ask themselves the same question, to tease out answers at *their* level. Here is a process for thinking through your Critical Areas (I am indebted to William Russell for the initial idea). It is set out for the head of a company or division but applies with appropriate changes at any level.

Ask yourself four simple questions:

1. Who is the decisive customer?

A car maker sells to a franchised dealer who sells to you and I. We determine the ultimate demand and are therefore the real customers. Teachers sell their skills to schools, who organise and distribute their deployment with pupils; the ultimate buyer is the state or public school parent. The latter may in the long run be decisive but it is the schools' needs which have the immediacy. It is they who must be impressed now.

2. What is the perceived product?

What does the decisive customer perceive as valuable in the product he identifies as yours? I used to smoke and occasionally bought tobacco from Dunhill in London. The company was then small; it *could* be described as a tobacconist but that quite fails to recognise the ambience, the range of choice, the product range, the advice and service that surrounded the purchase of the weed – accretions on the basic product which distinguished Dunhill from a straight 'tobacconist'.

Does a university manufacture degrees or education, to provide qualifications or to inculcate a mental discipline or to produce a 'rounded education' and 'personal development'? Perhaps the product varies with the student and is a mixture. I suspect a distinction should be drawn between products only a university can offer and those – e.g. degrees – obtainable more widely. In either case we are identifying customer perceptions and values as it is these which can make or mar sales. We have to know what they view as the real product they are buying. My company's sugar substitute means we are really selling will-power.

3. Why does or should the customer buy from you?

I used to buy Volkswagen Beetles and primarily for their reliability as I suspect did millions of others; the car was basically obsolete so VW simply had to maintain quality come hell or high water to command my continuing allegiance. I choose a particular personal computer primarily for its friendliness. To identify the primary attractions in your product, which distinguish you from similar suppliers, is to determine the essential qualities which by definition must be secured and preserved – price, styling, quality, or whatever.

117

4. What characteristic product attributes demand your personal attention?

This question is really embracing a more fundamental one – how do we make the product perceived as desirable by the customer at a profit? You have identified the qualities that must be embodied. Some attributes may derive from basic management functions – like production scheduling or quality control – and may probably be safely left to departmental routine. Or may not. If quality really is critical you will invest some of your own time in managing it. If price is a determinant, are cost controls or efficiency campaigns or R & D projects in need of your special attention because they cross departmental boundaries and may otherwise suffer from interdepartmental friction?

A Vice-Chancellor may think the university's survival depends in the short term on state funding and in the long term on its students' views of their university and on the community's respect for its products. While a mass of administration and teaching can be left to bursars and the faculty, attention to other areas may be mandatory – as we see below.

The final output from this process is a (probably quite short) list of critically important management activities that depend for their successful accomplishment on your personal attention. By definition, the time to deal with these MUST be found. The urgent must not be allowed to divert effort from the important.

Professor Sir Michael Thompson was Vice-Chancellor of the University of Birmingham. He thought it in need of drastic change. Here, quoted by David Walker in *The Times*, are some of the areas to which he gave special attention.

It is essential that the Vice-Chancellor involves himself personally in the appointment of all professors. He has to have a strategic vision of the important areas to develop. Appointing professors is the most powerful mechanism of change.

Allocation of resources between faculties, staff numbers, central direction, expansion of student numbers – these too deserved his time. The result has been growth with quality.

Here are two men with very clear priorities. At the Battle of Waterloo at the height of the fighting, the Duke of Wellington was commanding in his usual hands-on manner when he was accosted by a very brave salesman:

> During the fighting an enterprising Cockney commercial traveller astonishingly solicited his custom, 'Please Sir, any orders for Todd and Morrison?' 'No, but would you do me a service? Go to that officer (pointing), and tell him to refuse a flank (as told by J L Carr in his book *The Duke of Wellington*).

The Duke, as always, was not to be distracted from his prime objective – the defeat of the French. The salesman, conscious of his mortgage, must have thought the opportunity worth the risk.

Here is the Duke of Wellington again, still on the subject of priorities. At the time he wrote this letter to the War Office he was leading Britain's outnumbered army in the Peninsular War against Napoleon.

> Gentlemen, whilst marching to Portugal to a position which commands the approach to Madrid and the French forces, my officers have been diligently complying with your requests ... We have enumerated our saddles , bridles, tents, and tent-poles and all manner of sundry items for which [HMG] holds me accountable. I have dispatched reports on the character, wit and spleen of every officer. Each item and every farthing has been accounted for with two regrettable exceptions for which I beg your indulgence. Unfortunately the sum of one shilling and nine pence remains unaccounted for in one

infantry battalion's petty cash. And there has been hideous confusion as to the number of jars of raspberry jam issued to one cavalry regiment during a sandstorm in western Spain. This reprehensible carelessness may be related to the pressure of circumstances since we are at war with France. A fact that may come as a bit of a surprise to you gentlemen in Whitehall. This brings me to my present purpose, which is to request elucidation on my instructions from [HMG] so that I may better understand why I am dragging an army over these barren plains. I construe that perforce, it must be one of two alternative duties given below. One, to train an army of uniformed British clerks in Spain for the benefit of the accountants and copyboys in London. Or perchance, to see to it that the forces of Napoleon are driven out of Spain. I shall pursue either one with the best of my ability, but I cannot do both.

58 Using the Critical Areas' Concept

Several guides arise from identifying the matters demanding your personal attention (call them List A) and those major concerns, not for you but for your staff personally to handle (List B).

Now if List B really is critical at the level below you, then your surveillance, direction and control should logically concentrate on them. Equally, List B will bulk large in an appraisal of staff performance. The management information system, whatever else it does, must illuminate those critical areas The department's strategic plan, which is your concern, will certainly address those areas in List A. If managers lack the time to deal with them, being bogged down in routine or by their own helplessness, this *has* to be remedied.

To the extent it is used as a performance incentive, pay will reflect the importance of, and the performance in dealing with, the critical areas.

If the same critical areas recur on a list for a year or three, it may be that a simple course of pills is not enough. Managerial surgery may be called for. Alternatively, repetition may be signalling stability. Apparent omissions from List B should be checked; if you can't readily do this your ignorance is making you vulnerable.

I suggest there is yet another benefit from this whole way of looking at your department. To compose the list, itself a modest number of quite terse statements occupying at most half a sheet of paper, forces everyone to sit down and think through their business. Any fool can write twenty pages on his or her affairs; condensing all the evidence into a few words can only be done given 100% understanding, itself a function of hard thinking. As Robert Heller in *The Business of Winning says*, 'One of the brightest and best [ideas] . . . is that the essence of a manager's task is to think.'

59 Costing Products and By-Products

Here is no treatise on costing in all its aspects, only some practical points that have been derived from experience and from (other people's) hard thinking.

We want to cost something – a product or service or process, the first question is, for what purpose? To buy it from outside or from inside? To replace it? To modernise it? To sell it? To value it for insurance or to calculate its 'contribution' to total profit? All require differing assumptions and conventions.

The Lyle refinery at first made only refined sugar; later Golden Syrup was added. Instead of the non-sugars in the raw sugar that entered the refinery having all to be expensively separated from the sugar, if it were to be 'white refined', and sold very cheaply as molasses, some could remain – after purifying – in the syrup to confer flavour and colour and be sold very handsomely at Goldie prices. The refinery, so to say, now sells to the syrup factory a mixture of sugar and non-sugars instead of having to process the latter to molasses. Adding Goldie to the product range thus cheapened refined sugar. Was the saving to be credited to the sugar which was being benefitted or to the syrup which had created the benefit? We adopted the convention, which seemed entirely logical, of keeping sugar costs unchanged and crediting syrup with its benefit.

When I started in T & L we were exporting about a third of our total sugar output; having three refineries we might be able to say that one was effectively for export. We had always distinguished between home trade and export on the argument that the latter was much more competitive, difficult to forecast and less amenable to brand marketing – hence much more uncertain. How should we cost it? If we would really close a refinery were the trade lost it would be at total cost. If not, at marginal cost. We chose the second – with a qualification I shall come to later. We thought we'd never lose all or most of the overseas trade and to minimise distribution and other costs we would wish to maintain three refineries. In practice I suspect we could not then face the trauma of streamlining capacity so drastically.

T & L had for long had an elaborate and sophisticated system of product costing. All costs were distributed over all processes and each product – granulated sugar, icing, brown sugar, syrup, etc – was allocated its particular share of the process costs it incurred. Elements of expense were categorised into wages, materials (other than raw sugar), maintenance, depreciation, steam, power, and overhead. The last was analysed into departmental overhead and refinery administration in search of further precision. We knew quite accurately the costs incurred by a department for the canteen service, wages office, lab services, training, etc., thus 'Departmental Overhead'. This left the costs of overall refinery management, rates, personnel and costing offices, insurance, etc: this residue, 'Refinery Administration', was allocated arbitrarily to all processes pro rata to their total of other costs. This way of treating overheads was imperfect but did markedly improve on the conventional one of loading each unit with 50 or 100% of direct wages. Our arbitrariness was confined to around 20 or 30%.

For estimating cost changes or the cost of new processes or

products it was useful to have some simple ratios to guide us. Average ratios of each overhead element to total costs were fairly constant. Wages, materials, and energy could be estimated directly. As replacement value (RV) is a measure of size and complexity of plant (and was anyway needed by the accountants for the plant inventory) a control ratio is maintenance cost % RV. In T & L it varied between 4% and 8% per year. The maintenance expense on a new plant could thus be derived. Depreciation is a function of company renewals policy and the industry's rate of obsolescence. We distinguished between plant depreciation, usually 4% pa (a 25-year life) and building depreciation, usually 2% (a 50-year life).

An aid in estimating is to assess the effect of output on costs. Chemical engineers expect the ratio of costs to be in proportion to the 0.6 power of the ratio of outputs. This formula gives these indications:

Ratio of outputs:	2	4	6	8	10
Ratio of costs:	1.5	2.4	3.0	3.6	3.9

The predicted economies of scale are very striking. While inanimate plant costs may obey the rule, the managerial costs may not be so subservient – humans flourish in small environments.

The weak part in the system was estimating capital costs. Budget over-runs often rivalled that for the Channel Tunnel and were due to many reasons, all bad – inadequate investigation of new conditions, lack of control, changes of mind, the usual excuses. There was always the temptation to be economical with the estimating as too high a price or too low a return would mean rejection. A running check on a project was offered by Mr David Fishlock in the *Financial Times* many years ago. He proposed plotting this ratio:

$$\frac{\text{cost spent to date}}{\text{original total estimate}} \quad : \quad \frac{\text{estimated cost to complete}}{\text{new total estimate}}$$

This plot could reveal such a rake's progress as to warn that another Concorde was being created. Where there is scope to halt a project, for example a research one, the measure could be salutary. Suppose, for example, a project was originally estimated to cost £4.8 billion – like the Chunnel; at various points new estimates of the total cost are made, giving these revisions:

Cost to date:	0	1	2	3	4	4.8	6	8	12	12.5
Cost to complete:	4.8	3.8	3	3	3	3.5	3.5	2.5	0.5	
Revised total:	4.8	4.8	5	6	7	8.3	9.5	10.5	12.5	

The next diagram plots the Fishlock curve – not a pretty sight with its 160% budget over-run. It should have followed the middle line. The discrepancy is painfully obvious.

The elements of expense worked through above excluded the cost of raw sugar. We did this because the latter would have swamped all other costs, being some 80 to 90% of the sale price. As raws were allocated physically to a particular refinery to suit shipping and storage convenience yet incurred different processing costs which were beyond a refinery's control, depending on their origin, by convention the cost of raw was equalised for all refineries.

One more point. Though simple, it seems many people do not use what accountants call 'contribution'. You add a product to the range. If sales revenue minus marginal costs is positive, even barely so, then to that extent it is making a contribution to fixed costs and profit and thus has value. In other words, you will be better off doing the business than not doing it unless and until your costs, which have been to date marginal, become more or less 'fixed' by time or other commitment.

60 Costing Export Products

We treated exports as marginal business for T & L. Home trade sales were the base load sales, bearing full costs; exports opportunistically

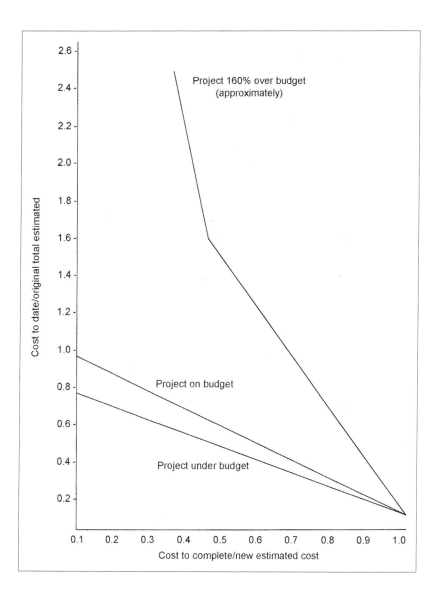

contributed marginal extra revenue for marginal extra cost. The underlying assumption inherent in these conventions is that if we lost all our export trade we would continue in business, albeit after some rationalisation; if we lost all our home trade we would have to wind up the company.

But export markets could be highly competitive. Just where and for what price did it pay us to sell? To elucidate this question required a complicated costing, though based on simple propositions: expenses at a given level of output can be separated into fixed and proportional elements by statistical analysis; 'fixed' costs will change if output varies *in the long term.* Thus to engage in an export trade was to accept an increase *over time* in some fixed costs:

Additional costs = extra output × proportional cost per tonne + calculated change in fixed cost

Most variable costs may be determined by basic statistics. Given a plot of expenses against output, which usually yields a scatter diagram, a 'regression analysis' (more can be learned of regression analysis from my father's book *Regression Analysis of Production Costs and Factory Operations*) will calculate the line of best fit of the form:

Cost (£) = fixed cost + output × proportional cost

The following diagram opposite shows this.

This technique does not disclose changes in fixed cost due to long-term changes in output.

We therefore had to use a theoretical approach which seemed to agree with what other data we had. We assumed that fixed costs broadly alter by the well-known chemical engineers' view that the costs of two plants vary as the 0.6 power of the ratio of their capacities. In practice in T & L's case we felt our changes were better covered by the 0.5 power. That formula gives this result:

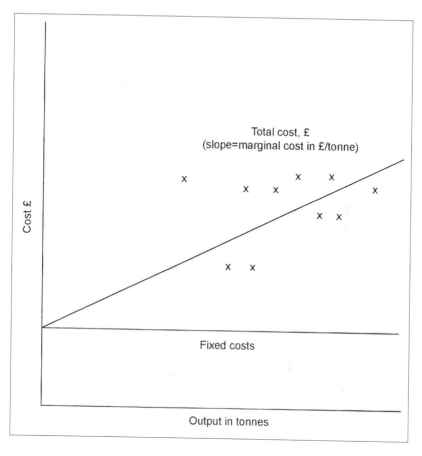

Index of output	0	50	75	100	150
Index of fixed expenses	0	71	87	100	122.5

We thus have estimates of the marginal cost incurred by additional sales and of the fixed cost increase this will generate over several years of business. The sum of the two elements gives the cost of 'routine' exports. Purely opportunistic business – one-off sales opportunities – can be treated as being of marginal cost type.

61 Basic Management Ploys

If we are clear on some straightforward managerial truths and methods we are less likely to be in need of or conned by management by panacea – 'Management by Objectives', 'Economic Value Added', or some other current fashion – which can be too limiting or enslaving .or ephemeral.

First, what do we do or what are we meant to do? We may or may not have been given a job description. If there is none this is an opportunity – we can fill the vacuum by commonsense, by what patently needs to be done. In any case we need to find out what if anything is expected of us and how much authority we really have. We must not interfere in departmental detail without good reason. We must have the time and the information to do those things only we as bosses can and should do. We must delegate to our staff and develop them. We must direct our unit – no one else can formally do so. If we neglect to do so, someone will step in and supply informal direction.

Second, we must set up and nurture a team. A person's responsibility should match his or her authority. Their job should be just within their ability. Outside it and they will be overwhelmed; too comfortably inside it and they will be bored or learn nothing. My first job in the Army was cleaning barrack rooms and loos. This was all right. Being easily and semi-automatically done I could think of other matters. (My dentist back in Civvy Street asked me, 'How did you get that job? Influence?') My second job was clerking. This became intolerable as it demanded my attention and bored me. One day I reached the bottom of my in-tray and to my dismay came on soldiers' personal records that had lain there undisturbed for over a year. I asked my boss, an amiable corporal, what to do. 'Meet me here after dark this evening.' We met, lit the stove to digest our paperwork and went back to the NAAFI. Silence reigns to this day. It was a lesson in initiative.

Delegation to the team is inevitable if an overload is to be avoided and personal development ensured. Delegation equals risk. Modem media exposure and investigative journalism make for playing safe and knowing everything that is going on. If a condom is apparently found in a packet of your product (T & L had just such a scare once) you know you will be criticised; if no contaminants are ever found you can expect no praise from the media. This must tend to over-burden the boss if he's not to be vulnerable and to under-load the subordinate. But the latter may be kept busy by exactly the same process at his level. The ultimate in delegation I have heard of is the flying instructor's sending his pupil off on his first solo.

It is much easier to define a team's individual roles fairly comprehensively than to have a free form organisation. The latter can work and may well nowadays be requisite to accommodate employees' aspirations but it calls for a high morale organisation where everyone will pick up any loose ends they spot, not leaving them to those ostensibly responsible, while not minding if this is done for some of their own tasks. Plaistow used to meet these exacting conditions and a free and flexible atmosphere was implicit. It worked very well, at least as well as in our Liverpool refinery which had the contrasting organisation, a manual laying down all possible detail. Honda's president makes the same point in *Fortune*. Commenting on a dearth of job descriptions and standards, he says,

> In times of growth that's good, because there is always too much for everyone to do. It's only when growth slows that you ask who does what.

It is always tempting to appoint one's subordinates' subordinate. We feel safer that way. If we yield to the feeling *we* are assuming the responsibility for performance, not the subordinate. British prime ministers do appoint ministerial assistants two levels down and then disown their accountability – thus a double whammy. The most we should do is reserve the right to veto a subordinate's choice. This is fair and necessary as it is the level at issue that supplies subordinates to *us* and we need a reasonable supply to choose from.

I believe in managing in part by walking around. It is however easy to get involved and give an order two or more levels down. On the other hand you can learn what is really going on, get a feel for morale and listen to comments on peoples' abilities – all valuable information and guidance. I was brought up to believe that all by-passing was wrong. I am now convinced it is not but should normally be limited to solving a crisis or gleaning critical information. We saw in section 31 how, in the Great War, Germany was concentrating on invading France while a thin screen of troops held off a Russian invasion, how the local German commander panicked, and how he was by-passed and replaced – for a huge and decisive battle. The unorthodox methods turned a potential disaster into a gleaming victory.

62 Promoting

Elevation deserves infinite care. The job being filled is at risk. It is a stepping stone to further promotion. Our choice will be viewed as a test of our public policies – do we actually mean what we say about 'promoting on merit'? An incorrect choice attacks morale generally, the promotee's peers and others will become disenchanted. Jack Welch, CEO of GE for two decades, writing in *The Times* with an opinion underwritten by GE's sustained success, comments,

> Getting the right people in the right jobs is a lot more important than developing a strategy . . . We learnt that we could have the greatest strategies in the world. Without the right leaders developing them, we'd get good-looking presentations and so-so results.

Selection depends on knowing the candidate's current performance and on predicting his potential and its match with the future demands of the job at issue. We don't know directly his potential, we can only infer it. If his present work is done effortlessly this is a favourable signal. There are other pointers – an IQ beyond present demands, a wider unparochial attitude, peers' respect, subordinates' respect. There arise some penetrating questions. Has he trained a replacement? Has he used his authority and initiative? Has he developed his staff? How is he viewed by his customers – other departments he may serve or supply? Fair questions these . . . and useful pointers, but the whole process is inferential. We have to deduce future performance from present form. Field Marshal Lord Wavell makes this point more entertainingly, 'The best confidential report I ever heard of was also the shortest. It was by one Horse Gunner of another, and ran, "Personally I would not breed from this officer".'

We must beware of the person who appears better when viewed from above than from below. General Zhukov became Stalin's favourite general and trouble-shooter in World War II. Here is an historian's comment on him, taken from Albert Seaton's *The Battle for Moscow*:

> [He had] the Russian's inborn respect for brutal authority . . . He felt himself in no way answerable to his subordinates or his troops. The only criterion was success, and it was immaterial how this was achieved. He . . . was frequently a bawling, raging tyrant in the field . . .

Ultimately, the essence of the matter is *future* competence: how likely is it that she or he will do the bigger job well and, in comparison with other candidates, significantly better? Not at all easy to answer with conviction!

I have on occasion buttressed these demanding enquiries with a (perhaps unfamiliar) supplement. Mr X has fallen under the Clapham omnibus. Each of his immediate subordinates are automatically on the short list, or think they are, to replace him. I say to each member of the team privately, 'You yourself are a candidate. Excluding yourself, if *you* were making the appointment, whom would you choose?' Some did not exclude themselves when responding but described what they would do; all commented on their colleagues. All answers were more or less illuminating. In one case they caused me to select – very appropriately as it turned out – the least obvious candidate.

There can also be an independent judgement. Here is a naval example. Admiral William Cornwallis, C-in-C of Britain's Channel Fleet in 1805, is talking to that fictional and very competent up-and-coming officer, Horatio Hornblower, in C S Forester's *Hornblower and the Hotspur*.

> 'Don't you remember what is the last privilege granted a retiring Commander-in-Chief?'

> 'No, sir.'

> 'I'm allowed three promotions. Midshipman to Lieutenant. Lieutenant to Commander. Commander to Captain.'

> 'Yes, sir.'

> 'It's a good system,' went on Cornwallis. 'At the end of his career a Commander-in-Chief can make those promotions without fear or favour. He has nothing more to expect in this world, and so he can lay up store for the next, by making his selections solely for the good of the service.'

The essence of promotion is identifying potential talent. Here is an example of talent spotting. Napoleon was appointing to his staff a young student of war, Jomini, who had first to hand over to his successor, quoted by Brigadier Peter Young in *The Victors*:

> 'If your Majesty will grant me four days' leave, I can rejoin at Bamberg.'

'And who told you that I was going to Bamberg?'

'The map of Germany, Sire.'

'How the map? There are a hundred roads on that map besides the Bamberg road.'

'Yes, Sir, but it is probable that your Majesty will perform the same manoeuvre against the left of the Prussians as you did against Mack's right at Ulm, and as by the St Bernard against Melas' right in the Marengo campaign; and that can only be done via Bamberg.'

He got the job.

63 Staff Development: Switching People

I believe a prime part of every managerial job is the development of its staff. Obvious ways of doing this are: structured training, including 'staff college' type courses such as Henley offers; a sabbatical; delegation; coaching. Far more than in industry, the services switch people from job to job. While a mere two years' posting sounds too short, the principle of rotation must be sound and industry does not do half enough of it. The Economist only a year or two back quoted a survey of business practice, 'Only one in 10 of the British firms interviewed switched managers around to give them experience of different parts of the business.' Mobile people do it for themselves by switching employers. The education and broadening that results can be seen in the product. Our people can be rotated between similar jobs – or even through those not so similar. My Personnel Manager proposed that a Refinery Manager and the subsidiary's Finance Director exchange places. I found the necessary courage and the roles were swapped. It worked out very well and refreshed and improved two good men. I admit I would never have thought of such a changeover for myself.

Rotation need not be confined to individuals. Teamwork has always been important; with decentralised authority – nowadays 'empowerment' – it is perhaps more so. It deserves to be purposefully nurtured. A well-rounded and cohesive team, where the whole is greater than the sum of the parts, can be switched as a complete unit to another situation. Complementary pairs are a specific example of a team. Military history is full of fruitful combinations: Marlborough and Eugene, Lee and Jackson, Hindenburg and Ludendorff, Montgomery and de Guingand. Their demonstrable performance assured their continuing partnerships throughout their respective wars. Where industry does find a team – manager and PA/secretary must be a frequent example – its permanence should be encouraged.

I have called development a duty. It is also a pleasure. I had a very competent secretary who was interested in filling an office management role then becoming vacant; the office manager discouraged her from promoting herself but I told her she could certainly do the job. She did. Some years later she went on to become Personnel Director of a large PLC, with other institutions to follow. A very modest push had born very satisfying fruit.

Deriving satisfaction from developing one's staff has been described as one of the (very few) essentials for a good manager of people – as opposed to being a manager of a business operation. In *The Times* recently Mr Desmond Dearlove reported in this fashion:

> British companies – in common with most Western firms – have a tendency to reward managers for current performance with little regard for the managerial legacy of tomorrow. As a result the ability to nurture subordinates is probably the most undervalued of all management skills. Yet only by developing the next generation's talent can companies hope to survive.

Being motivated by this satisfaction is needed when development through delegation involves risk. While you can't put the company in hazard by entrusting your project manager with complete freedom there must be some element of confidence demonstrated if he is to perform and to justify his salary, freeing you in the process to meet the other demands on your time. As a reward, you may be pleasantly surprised by your peoples' ability, given their head. Here is an account of an incident by the CO of a battalion serving in Bosnia, described by Colonel A D A Duncan, DSO, OBE in *The Rusi Journal*.

> One of my lieutenants was driving his Warrior [armoured car] along . . . and General Praliac, then a Croat General, came round the corner and ran his Colt Shogun straight into the front of the Warrior. The Shogun's front end was severely damaged. Praliac leapt out brandishing his pistol and shouting and screaming against everybody. The subaltern took his helmet off, climbed out, fetched his interpreter and said, 'General, I don't know what you're doing, but officers should not behave like that. Put that pistol away, calm down and behave like a gentleman'. The general put his pistol away and calmed down.

64 Practical Leadership

There is an imbalance in industry to be corrected. Sir Alistair Frame, then Chairman of RTZ Corporation, said:

> . . . Business schools tend to play down the importance of leadership in large corporations, and invariably stress management skills rather than leadership. I am sure that exactly the opposite is true in large projects, and possibly in business as a whole.

A conventional analysis of managing used to list these elements: planning, leading, organising, controlling . . . these four, and the greatest of these is leading. There are numerous extant studies of leadership. Here I have a few practical points which I suggest deserve attention.

There are copious arrays of attributes leaders should possess – vision, moral courage, determination and so on. I suggest it is more useful to clarify what leaders do. Here is an uncontroversial list.

- Give the team or unit a sense of purpose, to match the aims of individuals and the company.

- Provide the means to achieve the corporate purpose – team coordination, authority, money, skills.

- Convey a sense of achievement, of progress, towards the goal.

- Provide personal care and fair reward for individuals.

- Combine teamwork with its sense of belonging with a feeling of individual self-determination.

- Provide the inspiration that brings out superior effort.

Leadership, then, will have been exercised when the unit has achieved or is achieving its testing purpose despite substantial obstacles, while it feels rewarded and cared for, cohesive yet individualised. Ideally all these aspects are looked after; in practice some more or less incomplete combination can work. A keen sense of purpose and personal inspiration can offset severe deprivation, as Hitler demonstrated in the second half of World War II. Stalin would not score very highly for personal care and teamwork but the KGB and the cellars of the Lubianka compensated for his deficiencies. The son of the railwayman who contributed mightily to the loading and transport of hundreds of factories from the Ukraine to behind the Urals, to escape the German advance in 1941, told me that Stalin used to telephone factory managers there at two or three in the morning, expecting them to be at work and to hound them and terrorise them into dismantling their factories. 'No one else could have done it.' The father's reward was unexpected. On the day of the victory parade in Moscow he was arrested and sent to a concentration camp.

'Why?'

'No clear reason!'

'For how long? I asked.

'Oh, not long . . . eleven years.'

Field Marshals Slim and Montgomery in their very different ways performed superbly as leaders. Air Chief Marshal Harris, in charge of Bomber Command in World War II and Field Marshal Haig, commanding the British army in France in the Great War, both secured sustained selfless effort in the teeth of very severe casualties, even though both were physically remote and personally not very inspiring. Leadership can come in all shapes and sizes.

It must also be true that the individual's satisfactions – a feeling of purpose and achievement, of being in an elite, of gaining promotion and power – must exceed by some margin his 'costs', measured in terms of danger or long hours or physical hardship or stress; only with this perceived 'profit' will his allegiance be forthcoming.

In a quite real sense a leader operates by courtesy of the governed. They offer loyalty, cooperation, effort, *provided* he cares for them or obtains for them at least their fair share of corporate resources. That in their view is what he is there for. If he secures more than their share that is a bonus. 'I must follow them,' said Bonar Law, then British prime minister, 'I am their leader.' When Winston Churchill left the Government in 1916 he commanded an infantry unit on the Western Front. His men very soon enjoyed the best of clothing and equipment. It follows that loyalty cannot be demanded, it can only be earned – something that John Major as prime minister appeared to have had no conception of. Leaders may persuade or cajole or drive but in the long run they must articulate the feelings of the organisation or create a consensus about what is to be done. Major appeared to think leadership consists in stubborn adherence to some policy, despite any flaws becoming evident, and demanding unanimity for it.

Here is an example of effortless leadership, taken from *The Royal Navy. An Illustrated Social History* by Captain John Wells. The formidable Admiral Sir William Fisher was C-in-C Mediterranean Fleet when Marine Bugler McCarthy, age 15, his ship moored alongside the quay in Malta, was on deck on watch one fine evening:

> 'Suddenly it dawned on me that I was quite alone . . . [when] I saw an officer . . . approaching the gangway . . . [with] one thick gold band and four normal ones . . . Being sure he was coming aboard I manned the side. Just me. Better than nothing at all, I thought.

> 'Good evening' . . . I saluted smartly . . . 'Good evening, sir.'

> 'Do you know who I am?' No room for lies. This lad is an admiral.

> Watch it. 'No, sir.'

> 'I am', he said, 'Commander-in-Chief of the Mediterranean fleet'.

> He asked me my name which put me more at ease.

> 'Where is the officer-of-the-watch?' he asked.

> 'None of my responsibility, sir', I replied.

> 'Good boy', he said. He enquired about everyone else . . . before he disappeared down the half deck hatch. Then all hell was let loose. The officer of the watch appeared like magic. An hour later the admiral re-appeared with our admiral and the captain; the side was fully manned . . . Our visitor was piped over the side and all seemed to end nicely. But no; on reaching the jetty he stopped, turned and faced us

all. Then he said 'Thank you, bugler, for welcoming me aboard and doing your job properly. I salute you.' And he did just that.'

Finally, leadership is a question of horses for courses. Perhaps only a monomaniac like Hitler with a messianic mission could have inspired Germans to fight long and hard through a terrible and disastrous war for a vile cause. One would not choose a Hitler to captain a submarine armed with nuclear missiles or a Boeing 747, where calmness, authority, and methodical attitude must rank high. To lead a fighter squadron or an advertising agency, someone with dash and personality is appropriate. The commander of the British Army in Germany, or of a vast health care company like Johnson & Johnson, must have flair and vision. In short, the top person must match what is underneath. As Churchill said, 'If you are the summit of a volcano the least you can do is smoke.'

65 Paying Chairmen – and Others

Should salaries depend on level only or on performance as an additional factor? I'm ambivalent. As an executive director I was paid the same as my peers. If pay had been varied by our relative performances I might have felt it fairer, anyway for a period (and provided my salary exceeded the average) but I didn't feel unfairly treated, even knowing that some did more than others. The services manage with broadly fixed rates for each rank and they don't lack for stress and responsibility, as colonels in Bosnia, admirals and generals in the Falklands, and these plus air marshals in the Gulf have vividly demonstrated.

This apart, industry (like all organisations) still has the problem of ranking. Do a research scientist and a depot manager and a confidential clerk share the same grade and hence have at least the same basic salary? An in-house rating scheme can answer this fairly easily and well and cheaply or a consultant will have an expensive and ready-made one on his shelf.

Such a study leaves the pay of the chief executive or chairman undecided. This nowadays appears often to be fixed by a Remuneration Committee considerably composed of NEDs, themselves often CEs of other companies. The outcome is salaries undetermined by supply and demand, which should be the ultimate test. Justification for rises much in excess of hourly-paid employees comes in the form of comparison with other countries. Are we really to accept that our CE or chairman would emigrate if his one million-pound salary plus share options plus pension plus perks were halved?

It used to be taught – by the Glacier Metal Institute of Management – that the comfortable and sensible differential between adjoining ranks' pay was some 30%. I don't see this as a rigid rule. Nevertheless, 'felt fair' differentials are unlikely to exceed 50 or so per cent. Graham Searjeant writing in the *Sunday Times*, quoted an Opinion Research Centre Survey of a weighted sample of 1000 employees. There was a surprising consensus about relative take-home pay, to be summed up thus:

Rank	Relative Pay	Differential
Unskilled manual workers	1	—
Skilled manual workers	1½	1.5
Craftsmen	1¾–2	1.17–1.33
Supervisors	2	1.14–1
Departmental managers	3	1.5
Senior managers	4–5	1.33–1.66
Top CEs and managing directors	8–10	1.6–2.5

As a top person's pay sometimes now reaches 100 times his workers', the consensus is not all that extensive. That said, I can find reasons to dispute the figures. The weighting of the sample was not defined; if inversely proportional to rank the flatness of the escalation is to be expected; the more junior you are the less the justifiable perceived increment for the chairman. I suggest craftsmen deserve a higher differential.

There is a deal of difference between being a pipefitter or bricklayer on the one hand and an electrician or instrument mechanic on the other. Our trade unions always resisted widening such differentials. The differential enjoyed by each rank over the one below is erratic; it should either be constant or lie on a smooth curve. There is some scatter around Glacier's 30% guideline. My own conclusions are:

- General opinion tends to erode differentials which real and often hard-earned differences in skill would justify;

- This is particularly noticeable for some craftsmen and managers;

- Top managers' current pay levels are very hard to justify nor is much convincing attempt made to do so: with a wave to the shareholders the noses just dip into the trough.

On this last point, industry's top salaries are way over those of ministers, vice-chancellors, and top civil and military service people. In what studies I have seen, they appear not to correlate with company performance. The outcome is a denigration of commercial practice and integrity. The top brass appears cynical. Why does it act so as to undermine the reputation and continuation of its own private enterprise system? Is this just the short-termism it so much dislikes in others or simple greed?

Not necessarily. Chairmen defend the reward levels by reference to the talent market. But this merely adduces that all levels are argued to be high, not that they should be high. The Economist recently analysed this proposition. There are factors now making for high rewards at the top which simply did not apply in my day. Here are several.

It can be argued that top jobs are simply much more demanding than previously. This has to be correct. While post-Thatcher Britain reduced trade union power very considerably, other pressures more than compensated . . . consumer awareness and demands nurtured by the media and legislation, the severity of competition in many industries, staff demands for 'empowerment', City performance expectations, employment and product legislation, peer competition, technological complexity, simple but critical and often ignorant publicity . . . the list is formidable. The expectations for behaviour or results are not only hugely inflated but often ridiculous. Examples range across the scale. It may be wholly misleading to judge a firm's performance by quarterly or half yearly reporting. Some industries' life cycles are simply not that short. Information Technology and similar innovations require serious understanding and imaginative application. And new legislation intervenes – it is apparently not allowed now for a worker to lift more than 25 kg! A farm lad and I, also a lad, back in 1947 loaded 40 tonnes of wheat in 110 kg bags onto a high truck. We are still alive.

While many satisfactions may still be available in the work place, this downside is a serious deterrent. No wonder recompense is sought. Top job seekers need enhanced compensation when their predicated competence levels are much higher. If jobs are now more demanding, what of the supply of individuals able to fill them? Clearly the pool of talent in Britain must be much as in my day 25 years ago, except that more women are now willing and able to be candidates and more talent is mobile between countries. As the number of women and foreigners in top jobs is still modest we must reckon the supply is not keeping up with demand. In simple economics there are more buyers than sellers, so prices rise.

If numbers are rationed relative to demand, is quality or ability compensating? The education system is not different in principle, even if different in degree, than previously. An obvious change is the huge increase in business schools offering management courses and MBA degrees. It can only be a subjective view but I cannot see improved training doing much more than giving executives some assurance in dealing with modern managerial exigencies without much reducing the stress, the responsibility, the versatility, that they must confront.

Another factor may be investor pressures. Such overwhelming emphasis is now exercised on Boards for superior financial performance, based on short-term criteria as well as competitive forces, that they in self-defence seek 'winners' to give them that (possibly quite small) margin over the herd. If high talent is the norm, then very high talent is still more valuable. It can and will in today's conditions set its price.

And there may also be an element of opportunism. . Society has now different standards and motivations. Not to be prompted by these or to refrain from taking advantage may be a council of perfection. That it may offer only short-term benefit if it is perceived as selfish may only be natural when managers are doers rather than thinkers.. .

66 The Executive Pay Ratchet

Increasingly senior executives are being paid princely salaries, often boosted by bonuses and share options. Thus a top man, not necessarily the topest, may receive 60 times the annual reward of a labourer. *His* boss may receive 150 times the pay! *Fortune* magazine, designedly for business people, recently analysed (*The Great Pay Heist* by Geoffrey Colvin) the mechanism that generates such numbers.

The process involves company compensation committees. These typically are composed of non-executive directors, nominally unbiased, set up to determine seniors' remuneration with apparent impartiality. If they know about salary levels, this may well be because they are themselves top executives in other companies so not without a vested interest. If they don't know, specialist consultants are happy to advise, being equipped with data for many industries, and so able to transform trends into reality. For the Board, an apparently independent body is deciding pay . . . a picture that may convince the superficial shareholder . . . while actually doing its dirty work for it.

The *Fortune* article describes a ratchet at work. This proceeds by mechanistic stages:

1. A poorly performing company replaces its (apparently inadequate) CEO with a seemingly tested newcomer. He has to be offered a signing-on bonus to cover his forfeit options previously coming to him. His salary should of course exceed that of his (now incompetent) well paid predecessor.
2. Compensation consultants note his bonus and pay and the median remuneration for the industry is marked up accordingly.
3. Boards' Compensation Committees recognise this and inflate their salaries accordingly, typically aiming to be in the 75 percentile.
4. 'We cannot just be average, can we?' – so the average and the median for the industry are upped. Compensation consultants note this.
5. The typical CEO, often if he as well as his company is under-performing, gets more share options '. . . to motivate him to get the company's share price up.'
6. Other compensation committees have to allow for this increase when determining their pay levels.
7. The company becomes dissatisfied with the results and decides to replace its seemingly inadequate CEO.
8. When the CEO is sacked – for not all can be top performers and the pressure for a good company rating is ever increasing – he leaves behind him a big pay package, so his replacement needs a differential and an incentive . . . back to Stage 1!

Enough said.

67 Managing Company Cars

This is not the trivial subject it may appear. Company cars cost interesting money to buy and run; recipients value them highly; they connote status and rank so are doubly prized; those excluded from the handout are jealous of those not.

In my time T & L awarded cars nominally on need but in practice on seniority. It was then a very valuable perk, particularly when an excess of socialism raised the marginal rate of income tax to 75%, making the maintenance of proper differentials at all levels difficult or impossible. Subsequently, Conservative chancellors steadily eroded the value of the perk. I trust that the election of a Labour Government will not cause them and industry the deepest regret (written pre-Blair . . . some hope!)

I like the 'cafeteria' principle for perks: the individual can choose more or less for himself or herself pension or car or insurance or assisted house purchase or . . . etc. He can suit his personal needs while the company does not have to define rules and regulations laying down who gets what, when and how. This saves much management time and avoids creating perceived anomalies and invidious comparisons.

Recent experience in the car business tells me that the company car fleet needs managing by a professional, who can be an insider or an outsider so long as he knows the trade. There is much scope for applying skill and knowledge in buying and selling and in the control of costs. If a car leasing company or similar organisation offering complete fleet management looks expensive then employ your own specialist full-time insider. T & L didn't and paid for it.

There is still feeling about 'foreign' cars. It is partly a matter of opinion and image but sadly British is not inevitably best or most economic. Furthermore, commercial organisations with an export business should be wary of preaching against international trade. But I respect individuals' prejudices here though they should be clear about them. A woman once abused me for buying a foreign car.

I said: 'What car have you got?'

'We have a Ford Granada.'

Me: 'Why do you, being British, buy a car made by an American company in Germany?' She was very angry.

Car insurance was handled and paid for by the company; as with maintenance one was under no obligation or pressure to minimise its (considerable) cost. Now this expense can't be sneezed at. But then things were different.
Consider this Autocar report:

> . . . Gerard Gasson, a French schoolmaster, set out on 18 March 1976 in his forty-year old Citroen . . . to make insurance history. Approaching a railway crossing he skidded . . . and stalled across the track. He and his wife dismounted to telephone a warning, just as the automatic gates came down for the arrival of an express goods train. The train driver and his assistant jumped for it as the locomotive gathered up the ancient Citroen, carried it along the track, tearing up some 100 metres of it, left the rails and plunged into the Rhone-Mame canal, taking with it 21 wagons [carrying] beer and tinned soup, killing hundreds of choice roach and bream by shock, electrocution, or inebriation. For nine days all rail traffic had to be diverted, the canal had to be drained and repaired. The bill [was] probably the most expensive private car accident in the history of European motor insurance. The total estimate is £3.5–4 million [say c. £20 million in today's money] to pay for one locomotive, 21 freight wagons, one bridge, 100 metres of track, hiring 60 buses [and] cranes and equipment, compensation for 40 barge owners unable to follow their occupation, claims by the owners of the beer and soup, and claims by

the local anglers' society for lost catches. The train driver and his assistant are also claiming for broken ribs. M. Gasson has been advised that his premium will go up by 12½% to £22.50.

68 Managing Research

You will be pressured to fund a research programme: it demonstrates progressiveness; you can be labelled 'innovative'. You can also wave it at the media when your product is attacked for allegedly hurting people or the environment. This apart, scientists yield to no one in their ability to prod or shame sponsors into paying for their pet projects; increasingly they can use health or safety considerations to buttress what may be a suspect case.

Investment in (successful) research may or may not yield you a worthwhile dividend compared with buying in know-how or contracting work out or copying leaders on a 'me-too' basis when they can pay the development bill. It depends on circumstances. The point is, there are alternatives to choose from. Research is not the only route to innovation

In-house work particularly needs guidance, evaluation, motivation and control. The last is the most elusive: who can predict the (possibly high) worth of 'pure' research or the (probably limited) payoff of 'applied' work? For example, when we heard the sound of the very first Sputnik pinging round in earth orbit, who would have predicted that its first commercial application would come but two years later?

I think research is often largely faith, to be buttressed by finding a superb director for it. This is the first lesson. He won't be any more controllable than an uninspired person, probably less so, but by recruiting and stimulating good people and guiding them with sensitivity, insight and shrewdness he will maximise the chances of finding something new. If you go on long enough the result may be useful enough to be exploited in-house or sold outside, the latter being an option that may be unpopular but sound – you try to exploit an invention lying outside your area of business knowledge at your peril. We tried – and failed.

I worked with three T & L directors of research. One was a very knowledgeable chemist; he produced some new knowledge but of trivial value. Another was a practical refinery man; some good work occurred but despite his system, not because of it. The third, Professor Chuck Vlitos, was splendid. Supremely inventive himself, he could similarly coach and encourage others. Being self-confident, he could happily recruit able people. With his political sense he could design and broadcast effective departmental PR. With his ebullience he could ensure his lab was widely known and recognised which pleased its inmates. Being unparochial he kept in touch with useful labs and people world-wide and encouraged mutual aid.

He paid lip-service to control but in practice almost evaded it. This mattered much less than it might have done. He didn't equate size with success. The lab was substantial but by general industrial .standards quite small. This noticeably enhanced performance and is our second lesson. The lab had to make do with what it had – and did so.

Chuck understood human nature:

Most research groups . . . are characterised by two distinct personality types . . . defined as 'pioneers' and 'settlers'. The 'pioneers' are imaginative, creative, inventive and restless individuals . . . They resent too much authority or interference. They may come to work late but may often work at odd hours. 'Settlers' are happiest when assigned to clearly defined repetitive analytical tasks. They are easy to manage [and] are as vital to the research group as 'pioneers' but there is an optimum ratio of 'pioneers' to 'settlers' of about 1 to 5 . . . Once every 50 years or so individuals appear who combine the traits of 'pioneer-settler'. Marie Curie was one of these. Many Nobel Prize winners possess this unique combination.

Chuck also writes in his book *The Human Element in Research*, 'If the results of research are predictable the pay-off is correspondingly small. The more unpredictable the research the greater is the pay-off. Such long shots require the optimum exploitation of the unexpected result.'

Latterly an alternative to DIY research became apparent. Much of T & L's work could be farmed out to this or that university or institutional lab, chosen for its being a centre of excellence in its particular niche. This could be highly cost-effective. We could choose horses for courses and the labs need only charge us at marginal cost. To make it work would have needed a director with the knowledge, scientific credentials, personality and judgement to identify, organise, motivate and monitor all the outsiders – in short a Vlitos. We never tried this in my time. We should have done so.

A variant on this is to contract out or to detach part at least of your research to a foreign lab. For example, we considered transferring our synthetic chemistry work to an Indian lab with which we had a relationship. India has talents in that discipline. Costs could be low. The same argument applies to Russia with its wealth of educated ill-paid people.

69 Mechanisms for Innovation

Few companies can maintain whatever inventive spirit they start with through natural *élan* for very long. Fortunately there are devices to extend the initial impetus or to reinvigorate the constipated organisation. Some have been touched on: senior peoples' influence, listening to lively subordinates, employing young Turks, designing a vigorous research facility. These aids will (sadly) seldom suffice.

A central research laboratory may conduct itself to its own satisfaction but decentralising R & D focuses attention and creates stimuli from the market place. If the outcome is too short-term and neglectful of basic investigation, local units can commission this work – if given credit by top management to pay for it – or they may be given it free by a centrally financed lab, itself either in-house or contracted out. A Swedish company, Perstorp, supplemented these arrangements with a 'Managing Director's Fund' to finance risky projects and with the creation, said the *Financial Times*, of an '. . . ideas ombudsman . . . a spokesman for people with ideas, a sounding board, a source of contacts and a link man within the company.'

That large company, 3M, employs similar devices. An individual with an idea can try it on his boss; if that seems like a dead end he is free to try his luck with the Research Laboratory. Alternative channels for exploring new proposals must help sow a fresh harvest. The company's general principle is, Thou shalt not kill a new idea. This is given public credence by flexible costing – sometimes a department is not debited with development costs until it is able to bear them. Its management may be judged in part on its inventiveness.

The grass may be fresher in the next valley. T & L for many years employed full-time a senior technical man with a roving commission. He was encouraged to tour all our own refineries as well as others world-wide in search of new refining techniques and to make invidious comparisons. Latterly he worked half the year at Plaistow and half in an American refinery. With a base of knowledge and detailed briefing, his determination and keenness created continuing stimuli in top management to look, listen, adapt and improve. His character enhanced his theoretical value. No great diplomat but clearly kindly, selfless and enthusiastic, he could grip an audience better than a more polished operator might have contrived. He could also be irresponsible. In a power crisis at Plaistow he was found standing on a steam safety valve, in order to over-ride at some personal risk the boilers' quite satisfactory control system. People like that get listened to.

70 New Product Regulation

I was involved with the development of T & L's new low calorie sweetener, *sucralose.* This has all the characteristics of its ideal type: it has sugar's taste and sweetness *'profile'*, is heat-stable, is sugar-based so seems a quite 'natural' product but provides no calories. It was this fine combination of qualities which justified its development for the very competitive sweetener market. An essential ingredient of this scheme was obtaining the approval of the Food and Drug Administration (FDA). We originally thought this might take several years and we hoped for success in 1987. T & L twenty years later was still trying for it. A ex-colleague said to me, 'Would we have undertaken development if we had foreseen this extremely costly delay?' He had a point.

The FDA is US-based and has a political dimension. Furthermore, its role is complicated by an ill-informed public. Its officials know they will be heavily criticised if they approve a new product which turns out like thalidomide to have serious side-effects; they probably doubt if they will be praised for approving a safe beneficial new product. Thus the game for them has simple rules. Play 200% safe.

The outcome, typically ten plus years and a million pounds to get approval, must be to inhibit the bringing out of new beneficial products, to abort good ones with some but tolerable side effects and to delay progress in general. People who wish to risk the side-effects to find a better treatment may not be allowed the choice. And to cap it all, the public does not end up with complete safety. It does not realise this. It appears not to know that it is being sold short. In fact the media make headlines out of side-effects. The public is not told that *no* test programme can guarantee 100% safety. Humans and their environments are so complicated and varied that it is not possible to cover all possible contingencies in the lab, however many wretched test animals are maltreated:

151

The mouse is an animal which, killed in sufficient numbers under carefully controlled conditions, will produce a Ph.D. thesis.

Paraclesus pointed out years ago that everything is poisonous – the only issue is the dose.

Public awareness and education to strengthen politicians' will could in theory create a test system balancing reasonable benefit against a reasonable level of risk. I shall be surprised to see this happen. There are vested interests. Of course companies like T & L want more prompt FDA sanction – but if too readily forthcoming the possibility of dangerous side-effects would frighten the Board silly. It too needs an intelligent balanced screening procedure. Another interested party is the health fad industry. A lot of scientists get paid for researching one small aspect of diet or one food type or one tiny part of human metabolism when the subject is inherently too complicated to produce definitive results without studies as extensive as the object of their scrutiny. (Hence Mark Twain, 'To eat is human, to digest, divine.') Hence too there are fashions – avoid fat, take certain fats, avoid sugar, smoke, don't smoke, drink, don't drink – which baffle the public and give a living to 'experts' to concoct, write about, advocate, criticise . . . I believe there may be only one sure guide – moderation in all things. Could any headline be duller? By contrast food has given birth to a wealth of witticisms.

We lived for days on nothing but food and water. (W C Fields)

A food is not necessarily essential just because your child hates it. (Katherine Whitehorn)

I'd rather have a full bottle in front of me than a full-frontal lobotomy. (*Graffito*)

What contemptible scoundrel stole the cork from my lunch? (W C Fields)

152

Many years ago at a T & L AGM a question was asked about the then recently reported danger of consuming saccharin, a very cheap sweetener of very long standing. At the time we had no evidence to condemn saccharin beyond what was already well known, and said so. We knew of no additional reason for avoiding it. I thought it was time someone stood up and played down what appeared to be speculative and unduly alarmist about a possibly dangerous food additive and that this might be the more convincing when we did so about a competitive product. It is surely time that the limits of the feasible are set out clearly for the public.

71 A Siren's Voice: Diversification

A company with cash burning a hole in its pocket is beguiled into thinking of spending it on acquiring a different business instead of giving it to its shareholders. Although taxation may inhibit the latter it might in the long run pay better than investing in strange operations which often yield too low a return so that the shareholders end up with much less than was hoped for. Apart from discounting failure managements prefer growth to excellence as size swells self-importance and remuneration. The lure is dangerous. T & L met unexpected trouble with its take-over of United Molasses (section 27) though in the longer term the acquisition has proved satisfactory. There are some salutary questions that a board may ask itself before falling for temptation:

How little diversification do we need to meet our objectives? How much can we manage? (The test for that is, do we know what to do if things go wrong?) In pursuing technological and managerial unity the test is, what can we do more skilfully than our competitors? Not, what do we mentally understand?

Diagnosing trouble confronted T & L with its opposed take-over of Manbre and Garton. The Garton starch factory was put in my portfolio. The day after the announced capture I visited the Garton factory in Battersea to meet its management. Facing a mostly sullen team now to be bossed by unknown, seemingly ignorant, outsiders, I felt a four-letter man. The team behaved in the event better than we deserved. It also transpired that the factory was run in effect by unions and communists. It really was. It took one of T & L's best managers, Jim Scott, whom I put in to replace the incumbent person – who was *very* intelligent but who had been prepared to abdicate control, perhaps because he was not supported – 18 months to sort out the factory. One persistent problem, manning apart, was process performance. Jim and I, both production men, were baffled, even though starch processing is fairly akin to sugar refining. Eventually I sought private advice from an old starch man outside the company. He said, find yourself a process manager who really *knows* starch; I know your man. He did. I met him privately. We clicked. Alfred Derde solved the difficulty quickly.

I can recollect only one really natural and heaven-sent diversification. The family of Thurn and Taxis acquired a monopoly position in the distribution of mail in mediaeval Germany. How expand naturally from that base? 'They opened the letters and read what was in them. Thus they were able to run an espionage service and a news agency as well.' (Lord Hugh Thomas, *An Unfinished History of the World*).

72 Size or Excellence?

Shareholders beware! Your managers may just pay lip service to your rewards, even though you own the company. They have their own interests, which may conflict with yours. Managements may risk diversification in search of bigness, to expand their empires. This will be justified by forecasting theoretically attainable benefits which in practice often are mythical. 'Vertical integration', 'economies of scale', apparent similarity of businesses, all these are predicted to increase profits. Expansion within the industry is buying 'market share' or – less well advertised – 'neutralising competition'. Sharing R & D costs is favoured by the pharmaceutical industry.

So what are the real benefits? A KPMG 1998 study gave 17% of 'mergers' (though these may actually have been the strong buying the weak) as adding shareholder value and 53% as depressing it. Harvard Business Professor N Nohria thought only 30% of the top US firms had created positive benefit in 1985–95 despite numerous reorganisations. My memory of similar UK studies accords with this dismal picture.

Whiteley takes an illuminating view of this scene. He explains the phenomenon as due to, '. . . the gap between the accounts, which are used to justify a merger, and the reality. In a modern organisation the accounts record around 10 per cent of the value of a company; the people represent the other 90 per cent. Yet merger statements still focus on the 10 per cent. Worse, they announce an intention to damage the 90 per cent, by stating that there will be redundancies.' (From an article *A merger most foul* by Philip Whitely in *The Times*.)

The execution of existing staff may be done by broadbrush methods, thus losing the valuable with the dross. It may not be obvious to the new directorial broom that this older man is doing much but when a crisis hits, he's seen it all before and the cure can be instantaneous. Thus Whiteley sums up, 'Profits come from people, not structures, and it is on the development of people that successful strategies focus'.

Index

Allen, William: 38
Attfield, Michael: in United Molasses, 60
Bennis, Prof.: on CE's overload, 62
Blakstad, Michael: on down-sizing, 43
Bonar Law: on leading, 137
Bruce, Robert: on accountants, 32
BTR: 53

Canada & Dominion Sugar Company (C & D): and T & L, 54; Board composition, 54, 56; productivity of, 82
Capitalism: 68; in USA, 71; and democracy, 78
Careers: choice of, 109
Cars: 145
Chairman: role of, 46; changing, 49; paying, 139
Chief Executive: role of, 45; overload of, 62

Carmichael, John: as Chief Engineer, 33
Churchill, Sir Winston: and de Gaulle, 14; on executive power, 48; as leader, 137, 139
Clare, J (Chairman of J & J): 109
Clarke Shoe Company: 46
Colvin, G: 143
Companies: and democracy, 78
  See also DIRECTORS, FAMILY BUSINESS
Compatibility Ltd: 104
Computing: 27
Cornwallis, Adm W: 132
Costing: of products, 122; of exports, 126
'Critical Areas': concept, 116; application, 120

Dearlove, D: on nurturing subordinates, 134
de Gaulle, General: 14

Derde, Alfred: 154
Directors, Executive: 12, 47;
    remuneration of, 139, 143
Directors, Non-Executive: and
    surveillance role, 50; value of, 51;
    and United Molasses, 60; in
    remuneration committees, 140
Discounted Cash Flow (DCF): 87, 89
Diversification: perils of, 153
Duncan, Col. A D A: 135

Ellyatt, John: in Rotterdam, 6
Emerson Consultants: explosive effect
    of, 38

Fairrie, G: 58
Family Business: control of, 2;
    innovation in, 13; direction of, 13;
    recruitment in, 16; direction of, 13;
    family exclusivity, 45, 57
Federal Drug Administration (FDA):
    decision rules in, 109; regulatory
    role, 151
Fields, W C: 153
Fisher, Prof. R A: 37
Fisher, Adm Sir W: as leader, 138
Fishlock, D: on cost control, 123
Frame, Sir A: on leadership, 135
Fuel saving: 25

Gellerman, Dr Saul: 66
Glacier Metal Institute of
    Management: on pay differentials,
    140
'Goldie' (Lyle's Golden Syrup): output
    of, 2; and trademark, 99; can
    making for, 11; quality control of,
    12; costing of, 121

Goldsmith, Sir James: and the EU, 70
Goldwyn, S: 46, 96
Gorbachev: 69
Green, Sir Owen: on directors' pay, 51;
    on non-executive directors, 53, 67
Gregory, Dr R: at Plaistow, 38

Haig, F-M Viscount: as leader, 137
Hammerstein-Equord, General: on
    officers' attributes, 32
Harris, ACM Sir Arthur: as leader, 137
Hayek, F A von: on freedom, 71
Heller, Robert: on Value Added (VA),
    79, 121
Henry Tate & Sons: merger with Lyle's,
    2
Hesser Packing Machine: 22
Hiscocks, H M: and de Gaulle, 14
Hitler, A: as leader, 136, 139
Honda: 129
Hooper, Sir F: 32
Hornblower, Lt. Horatio: 132
Howe, Lord: and Lady Thatcher, 49

IBM: responsiveness of, 28, 29
innovation: in 3M, 150
Intelligence: 103
Internet: hazards of, 104; uses of, 104;
    security, 107
Ivens, Michael: on capitalists, 72

Jellicoe, Lord: T & L chairman, 49, 50;
    and management succession, 67
Jellicoe, Adm Sir J: at Jutland, 102
Johnson & Johnson: 109
Jomini, Baron A H: 132

Kalecki: on Value Added, 81

Keynsham Packing Station: efficiency
of, 22, 33
KPMG: 155

Lebowitz, F: on food in diets, 8
Levin, B: 8
Lyle, Abram: 1, 9, 45
Lyle, Charles (later Lord): as Sales
Director, 15
Lyle, Colin: and Army, 18, 65, 67, 71,
77, 82
Lyle Foods Ltd: 90, 94, 100
Lyle, Sir Ian D: in War, 14, 35; on
power, 47, 48, 56, 115
Lyle, John O: as T & L chairman, 49
Lyle, Sir Leonard (later Lord): 48
Lyle, Sir Oliver: on Tate merger, 2; as
Plaistow Director, 13, 15;
recruited, 16, 25; and Invicta cars,
29, 34; on design of experiments,
37
Lyle, Philip: on Tate merger, 2, 28; as
Plaistow Director, 13, 15; Hesser
purchase, 21; and Invicta cars, 29;
introduces statistical techniques,
36; and change of chairman, 49;
and costing, 126
Lyle's Golden Syrup: see GOLDIE

Macklin, Sir Noel: and Invicta cars, 29
Major, John: 137
Management: of refinery, 13; of
promotion, 18, 130; of production,
24; in Army, 32; and pairing, 34; of
training, 41; of Board, 46;
recruitment, 98; of company cars,
145; of research, 147; of
innovation, 150

See also FAMILY BUSINESS
Management Consultants: 38; case for,
40; McKinsey & Company, 38, 54;
in Marks & Spencer, 41
See also EMERSON
Maucher, Helmut (Neste CE): on
priorities, 116
McKinsey: see MANAGEMENT
CONSULTANTS
Molasses: production of, 3
Moltke, General Helmut von: in
by-passing, 65, 115
Montgomery, F-M Viscount: uses chief
of staff, 63; as leader, 137
Mueller, R K: 34
Napoleon: 64, 132
Nestle: see MAUCHER
Nicholson, T: 41
Nuclear Electric: 59

Operations Research: 30

Pay: Sir O Green on, 51
Perstorp: and innovation, 150
Petch, Adrian: as computer manager,
29
Peters, Thomas J: 35
Plaistow Refinery: 1; and nepotism, 2,
13; packeting, 22; and fuel saving,
25, 37, 38, 58; productivity of, 82
Private Enterprise: rationale, 68; and
freedom, 69; reputation, 72
Productivity: in can making, 11; in
Canada, 82
Profits: 'needed', 73; in public
perception, 74; not an objective,
76

Rees-Mogg, Lord: and EU, 70
Renewals (of plant): timing of, 85
Research: as a priority, 108;
    management of, 147
RTZ: 135
Runge, Charles: 45
Runge, Sir Peter: and A E Tate, 17, 45,
    48; and DCF, 90
Runge, Julius: 45
Russell, W S: 116
Russia: 69, 72

Saccharin: safety of, 153
Samson: 9
Scott, J C R: 154
Serjeant, Graham: 140
Shaw, Anne: 98
Shaw, Sir Neil: 54; as CE of C & D, 55;
    reconstructs T & L, 60
Slim, F-M Viscount: as leader, 137
Stalin, J: as leader, 136
Steele, Prof.: 62
Stewart, T A: on intellectual capital,
    83
Stiles, Chris: on older managers, 15; on
    management selection, 20
Sugar, beet: sweetness of, 4
Sugar, cane: cultivation of, 5
Sugar Refining: rationale, 4; packing,
    21; production scheduling, 24;
    creditors, 75
Sugar, refined: and health, 7
Sugar, UK refining company for: and
    profitability, 75; creditors, 75

Tate, A E (Long John): recruitment, 17;
    and OR Department, 30
Tate, F H (Tony): 49

Tate, J F P (Short John): xv; and
    cube-making, 34
Tate, Sir Saxon: as NED, 53; as CE of
    T & L, 67
Tate, Vernon: 49
Tate & Lyle Ltd.: origin, 2; and raw
    sugar factories, 4; and WSRO, 8,
    32; its Head Office, 46; Board
    organisation, 47; changing
    chairmen, 49; and NEDs, 50; and
    Canada, 55, 56; its CE, 67; and
    diversification, 59, 73; and DCF,
    90; and research director, 148; and
    innovation, 150; and FDA, 152
Thatcher, Lady: 49
Thompson, Prof. Sir M: and critical
    areas, 118
3M: 150
Training: managing of, 41
Twain, Mark: 152

United Molasses Company: take-over
    of, 59

Value Added (VA): definition, 79;
    division of, 80; as measure of
    efficiency, 83; increase of, 85; and
    high pay, 91
Vlitos, Prof. A J: on research
    management, 148

Waterman, Robert H: 35
Wavell, F-M Viscount: on appraisals,
    131
Welch, Jack: on informality, 36; on
    selection, 130
Wellington, Duke of: at Waterloo, 119;
    on priorities, 119

Wells, Capt. J G. RN: 36, 138
Whitehom, K: 152
Whiteley, P: on mergers, 155
Whitmee, J O: in Canada, 55
World Sugar Research Organisation:
    T & L membership of, 8, 9

Yonkers Refinery: 71
Young, David: 59
Young, Brig. Peter: 132

Zambia: cane growing in, 6, 34
Zhukov, General: character, 131
Zimbabwe: 34
Zuckerman, Lord: 30